THE LITTLE MAN

with the

LONG SHADOW

A Bur Oak Book

THE LITTLE MAN

with the

LONG SHADOW

The Life and Times of
Frederick M. Hubbell
by George S. Mills

University of Iowa Press
Iowa City

University of Iowa Press
Iowa City, Iowa 52242
www.uiowapress.org
All rights reserved
Printed in the United States of America

The University of Iowa Press is a member of Green
Press Initiative and is committed to preserving natural
resources.

Library of Congress Cataloging-in-Publication Data
Mills, George, 1906–2003.
    The little man with the long shadow: the life and
times of Frederick M. Hubbell / by George S. Mills.
    p.   cm.
    ISBN-13: 978-1-58729-541-6 (pbk.)
    ISBN-10: 1-58729-541-5 (pbk.)
    1. Hubbell, Frederick M. (Frederick Marion), 1839–
1930.   2. Businesspeople–United States–Biography.
3. Railroads–United States–History.   I. Title.
HC2754.H75 M55 1988
977.7'02'0924 [B]   88-13117

07   08   09   10   11   P   5   4   3   2   1

Contents

CHAPTER   PAGE

1   1855 1
2   By Stagecoach from Muscatine............... 6
3   Sioux City 15
4   Mary Wilkins 23
5   Hard Times 38
6   22 Important Years........................ 50
7   Narrow Gauge 61
8   Builders 68
9   Student of Railroads....................... 78
10 Polk & Hubbell........................... 93
11 Thrift 105
12 The Equitable 116
13 Health 125
14 Family 131
15 The City Council.......................... 143
16 The Hubbell Estate........................ 160
17 Terrace Hill 170
18 Poker 187
19 Color 196
20 Master of All Trades...................... 207
21 An Old Man............................... 223
22 1955 231
    Family Tree 240
    Sources 244
    Index 246

v

Illustrations

FACING PAGE

Frederick M. Hubbell in 1894........................VIII

F. M. Hubbell at 16............................. 14

Letter of application written by F. M. Hubbell........... 30

Page from the early Hubbell diary.................... 31

Phineas M. Casady............................. 46

Marcellus M. Crocker........................... 47

Jefferson Scott Polk............................ 62

An early train in Polk County...................... 63

Hoyt Sherman 78

Wesley Redhead 78

B. F. Allen 78

Gen. Grenville Dodge........................... 78

Demoine House 79

Mrs. Frederick M. Hubbell........................ 94

Family group picture taken about 1896................. 95

H. DeVere Thompson 110

Walnut Street before 1880.........................111

Early home offices of the Equitable Life...............118

Present Equitable home office......................119

(Continued on Page VIII)

ILLUSTRATIONS

(Continued from Page VII)

FACING PAGE

Frederick C. Hubbell.............................134

Grover C. Hubbell...............................135

Frederick W. Hubbell............................142

James W. Hubbell...............................143

Countess Beulah Hubbell Wachtmeister.................174

Terrace Hill 175

Albert B. Cummins..............................190

Charles S. Denman..............................190

Chester C. Cole................................190

B. F. Kauffman, Sr..............................190

James H. Windsor...............................191

G. M. Hippee..................................191

James Callanan 191

James S. Clarkson 191

Frederick M. Hubbell at about 75 years of age.............222

Frederick M. Hubbell with his great grandchildren..........223

Aerial view of present-day Des Moines.................238

FREDERICK M. HUBBELL in 1894.

About the Author

GEORGE MILLS is a newspaper reporter with a zealous interest in the present and a lively curiosity about the past. As a reporter for The Des Moines Register he writes about current affairs in Iowa with a skill and understanding widely respected among his colleagues. The perspective which his reporting gives to the day's events is in large part a reflection of his understanding of what happened in the past. Throughout his newspaper career he has been a diligent student of American history with a special interest in the political, economic and cultural development of Iowa from the days when Iowa was an open, sparsely settled prairie.

If he has brought a historian's point of view to journalism, he has also brought a reporter's viewpoint to history. He has been able to see the great and small figures of our past, not as museum pieces to be studied, but as living men and women to be understood in terms of the times in which they lived. He would seem to be, therefore, the ideal person to write a biography of Frederick M. Hubbell, who played such an interesting and important role in early Iowa history.

Like Mr. Hubbell, Mr. Mills was not born in Iowa but came here as a young man. A native of Chicago, he was graduated from Northwestern University in 1928 and began his newspaper work in Iowa shortly thereafter. He has worked for the Associated Press, the Iowa Daily Press Association, the Marshalltown Times Republican, and the Cedar Rapids Gazette. Since 1943 he has been a reporter for The Des Moines Register.

KENNETH MACDONALD,
Vice President and Editor
The Des Moines Register and Tribune

1855

A STAGECOACH CARRYING a 16-year-old boy and his father rolled into the little town of Fort Des Moines, Iowa, at 6 o'clock in the evening of May 7, 1855.

That was exactly 100 years ago today.

The coach took the travelers to the old Everett House on Third Street, south of Walnut Street, to spend the night. They had come from their home in Connecticut by railroad, steamboat and stagecoach. The father wanted some of that wondrous Iowa land he had heard about. The price was $1.25 an acre. The older man had $2,000 in gold. The boy had practically no cash. He had given his father his last $9, drawn from the bank back home, to help pay the expenses of the trip.

The father was Francis B. Hubbell. The boy was Frederick Marion Hubbell.

The next day the elder Hubbell rented a carriage and started west. He located a claim of 160 acres near Adel in Dallas County. The amount he paid for the 160 acres was $200. That sum would not buy a single acre of the same land today.

Young Fred stayed behind to look for a job in Fort Des Moines, which had a population of 1,500. In later years, he recalled: "Commencing at the south end of Second Street, I went into every store and office, but was told each time that they had no use for a boy. I came up Second Street to Court Avenue, up Court Avenue to Third Street, up Third Street to the hotel where we were stopping."

Near the Everett House was the United States land office for the Fort Des Moines District. The job-seeking youth went there next. Phineas M. Casady was in charge. He said he had no use for a "green boy." Casady nevertheless hired young Hubbell, perhaps on a hunch. The salary, agreed upon several weeks later, was $100 a year and board.

The "green boy" was destined to become: The wealthiest Iowan in the state's history; a founder of a great insurance company (The Equitable of Iowa); a railroad financier and builder who did business with such nineteenth-century rail barons as Jay Gould and Russell Sage; a public utilities magnate; a leading lawyer, and probably the most spectacularly successful investor in real estate that Iowa has ever seen.

Fred Hubbell died in 1930 at the age of 91. His life is a story of individual success in the good old American tradition. The properties that he accumulated are still largely intact within a trust that he created. Under continued expert management, the

Hubbell holdings have expanded greatly. Most of the property, both tangible and intangible, cannot be sold for many years to come.

The Hubbell fortune was built in Iowa, a rural state. Such an area usually is not looked upon as a likely location for colossal accomplishments in the business world. New York, Chicago or Boston, yes. But not agricultural Iowa.

How did Hubbell do it?

Above all else, he possessed a tremendous will to succeed. Starting with nothing at 16, he amassed $4,000 worth of real estate at 17. He served as acting Clerk of the District Court in Sioux City at 18. When he was 19, he was admitted to the practice of law. At 21, he helped found Sioux County, Iowa, and was elected Clerk of the District Court. At 27, he helped organize Des Moines' first streetcar company. At 28, he was the moving force in the organization of the Equitable Life Insurance Company of Iowa. At 32, he and his law partner organized the first Des Moines Water Company. He was deep in railroad building and financing before he was 35.

For all his triumphs, Fred Hubbell was a deeply human person. His diaries show that. The Hubbell diaries are among the most important Iowa historical finds of this century. He kept a daily entry diary most of the time from 1855 to 1927. He bought a diary book for each year.

Some of these books are missing now. And the pages in the surviving volumes often are blank. That is not surprising in a life as busy as Hubbell's. Also, the information in the diaries frequently is sketchy and incomplete. That is not surprising either. He did not keep the diaries for posterity. The daily record usually was kept for his own information and recollection.

Even so, the diaries contain, in his own handwriting, probably 250,000 words of insight into the life and times of Frederick M. Hubbell. (A little of it is in shorthand, which he taught himself.) The all-but-forgotten diaries have been stored in a vault in the Hubbell Building in downtown Des Moines since his death.

The diaries reveal his personal drive and determination, some of his love affairs, $1,000,000 deals and $2.50 transactions, pride in his family and home, joy in children born. Great men march through the pages of these little books. Railroads are born, built and are sold. Hopes rise and are crushed in the vigor of 19th century and early 20th century private enterprise.

As the diary years unfold, Hubbell is pictured as a thrifty individual and a difficult person to best in a bargaining session. At the same time, he spurned corruption. He refused to "pay off" receptive city councilmen when franchises came up for a vote. He was a hard man with a dollar in a business deal. But he quietly helped a family whose home had burned. He long was president (and a financial angel) of the Des Moines Home for the Aged.

He personally had a deep fear of being in want in his old age. He determined early in life that he would not be a burden on others in his declining years. He constantly was preoccupied with his health. And he was deeply interested in the subject of death.

The diaries disclose another little known fact about Fred Hubbell. He played poker regularly for small stakes. Over a quarter of a century, he kept track of every dime won or lost.

Hubbell was small physically, barely 5 feet 2 inches tall. He usually weighed 125 or 130 pounds. But he loomed large in the affairs of his time. His influence lives on strongly today, 100 years after his arrival in Des Moines. And the end is not yet. Through his highly competent descendants and through the instrumentalities he created, it appears entirely likely that the impact of his personality will be distinguishable in Des Moines clear up to the year 2000, and perhaps beyond.

He was a little man, but he cast a long shadow.

2

By Stagecoach from Muscatine

WHY WAS Fred Hubbell so determined to succeed? A 1925 newspaper interview provided one revealing glimpse into his personality. He was 86 years old at the time. He told the reporter: "When I was a little boy, the grownups shooed the children out of the room and then they talked about their neighbors. I wanted to hear about the neighbors. I used to hide behind the stove and listen hard with both ears. They often declared that some of these neighbors were headed for the poorhouse. I learned to have a real dread for the poorhouse and resolved that I would have some money when I grew old so that I could keep out of that dreary place."

These neighborhood conversations took place at Huntington, Conn., where Fred was born January 17, 1839. His father was a stone mason.

The boy attended country school until he was 13. In later years, he related: "I came home one night and told father that it was no use for me to go to school because the girl who was teaching the school did not know as much as I did. His answer was: 'Well, then you must go to Birmingham to school.' So I started to walk 3½ miles to Birmingham. I went to that school for about three years, until I was 16 years old."

He was always a top student. He constantly looked for ways to better himself. At his suggestion, a Birmingham teacher started a special class for those who wanted to improve their handwriting. Hubbell attended. All this time, the "poorhouse" talk weighed on his mind.

"Whenever I heard the neighbors talking, they discussed the imminent bankruptcy or ruin of this man or that man," he said. "Not long after I finished school, my father decided to come west. I wanted to get away from that depressing atmosphere, so I asked him to take me along. He didn't want to but I finally persuaded him. The west seemed to offer so much more for a young man."

A century-old picture shows 16-year-old Fred to have been a serious-minded, determined youth. His hair was long and he wore a large, ribbon-like bow-tie.

On April 30, 1855, the Hubbells left Connecticut for far-off, mysterious Iowa. They probably had no intention of settling in Iowa permanently. The father wanted to do a little speculating in land. As for young Hubbell, his goal in life was to attend West Point military academy. The pioneer west did not figure in his longtime plans.

"Started. Bid grandma farewell," the diary says laconically for April 30. The Hubbells reached Chicago May 4 and immediately boarded a train for Rock Island, Ill. There they took a steamboat for Muscatine, Iowa, the terminal for a western stage.

"Came down the Mississippi at 6 in the evening," the diary says. "Put up at the Irving." (Presumably a Muscatine hotel.)

There were no railroads west of the Mississippi to Fort Des Moines in those days. On May 5, the travelers left in a stagecoach for Fort Des Moines. It took a full day to reach Iowa City. They rode all night and all the next day. The diary says Fred felt sick and thought he "should have cholera." The elder Hubbell bought peppermint at Marengo for his queasy son. The other passengers left the stage at Newton. The Hubbells had the coach to themselves the rest of the tedious, bumpy, muddy way. They reached Fort Des Moines at the end of the third day.

Fort Des Moines (the word "Fort" wasn't dropped from the town's name until 1857) was still a small frontier settlement. The principal stores were on Second Avenue between Market Street and Court Avenue, south of the present main postoffice. East of the Des Moines River and north of Walnut Street were thick woods. Fort Des Moines had been an army post until 1846. The soldiers were gone in 1855 but their cabins had not yet been torn down. In fact, Barlow

Granger had started Fort Des Moines' first newspaper, "The Iowa Star", in one of those cabins in 1849.

There was an air of constant excitement in the little community in 1855. Steamboats frequently came up the river from Keokuk bringing supplies. The dock was at the foot of Court Avenue. Of much greater importance, however, was the unending stream of pioneer families plodding westward behind oxen and horses, seeking new homes. When he got a job in the land office, Hubbell found himself in the busiest place in town. The federally-owned land was available to settlers at $1.25 an acre. Hundreds of thousands of fertile acres lay everywhere for the asking. Dozens upon dozens of settlers came into the land office daily to enter claims and to pay over their painfully saved pieces of gold.

"Helped count out $25,000 for the first time," Hubbell wrote May 19, 1855. On May 22, he said: "Rather cool, wrote all day, had a very good business. Took in 15,000 dollars. Am going to have my hat washed and my clothes too. Reading a novel."

While reminiscing in his old age, Hubbell recalled: "Mr. Casady put me behind the counter and I recorded land sales. People were coming in from all parts of the country to buy cheap Iowa land. We were paid in gold and salted the gold pieces away in an iron box. At the end of each week, one of our men took the box by stage to Keokuk and went from there by steamboat to St. Louis where the government had a sub-treasury for the deposit of money. He never took less than $100,000 all in gold but I never heard of one of these men being robbed. Many people in the boat and stage knew of his mission and the fortune he carried. That was before Jesse James set the style in banditry."

Casady questioned Hubbell closely before giving him the job.

"Mr. Casady was a kind and understanding man," Hubbell said years later. "He examined me as to my education, age, where I came from. He asked me what I had studied. I told him I had studied Virgil and Caesar and knew algebra, geometry and trigonometry. Those seemed to be good qualifications for an office boy."

Isaac Cooper, who also worked in the land office, was dubious.

"Why did you hire that boy?" he asked Casady.

"You just watch that boy," the agent responded.

Both Casady and Cooper were to become very well acquainted indeed with Hubbell in the next dozen years. Hubbell and Casady were leaders in the organization of the Equitable. And Hubbell married Frances Cooper, Isaac's daughter. They lived together for more than 60 years, until her death in 1924. Isaac Cooper was a nephew of James Fenimore Cooper, the famous American novelist. All three of the children of Mr. and Mrs. Frederick M. Hubbell were given "Cooper" for a middle name.

When Casady first hired Hubbell, nothing was said about salary. Two weeks later, Casady asked the youth what he thought he ought to get. Hubbell answered: "Whatever you want to pay me." The discussion continued off and on for two more weeks.

"He (Casady) could get no satisfaction from me," Hubbell said. "I was afraid if I did not name a figure satisfactory to him that I would lose my job."

Casady finally took the plunge.

"Well, Fred, how would $100 and your board be for one year?" the agent asked. Hubbell agreed with alacrity. He was glad to get $8.33 a month in cash. He boarded at Casady's house most of the time that he worked in the land office. One of his first land-office customers was his father.

"When my father returned from Dallas County to record his land," Fred said, "he found me in the office waiting to make out his receipt and take his money. He had made a deal to sell his land immediately at an advance of 40% over the $1.25 price. I was convinced he was making a mistake but at 16 I didn't feel able to advise or persuade him. He wanted me to return to Connecticut with him but I had decided to remain in Fort Des Moines." Francis Hubbell did not go away and leave his son penniless. He gave the boy $5 in gold for working capital.

Fred was a lonely and homesick 'teen-ager in a strange new land the following few months. He wrote innumerable letters to relatives and friends back home. He never was satisfied with the amount of mail he received. On June 15, 1855, he complained in the diary that he had gone "down to the post office. Did not get anything. Should like to get a letter from someone."

He also wanted other work, probably because of the pay. On May 31 he went "to see the engineers. Could not get a job." He did not say who the engineers were. Fourteen hundred miles from home in a frontier town, the boy turned to his studies with new concentration. He had brought books with him from Connecticut. By himself in his room at night, the 16-year-old studied analytical geometry, French and trigonometry. Later he studied law, more Latin and shorthand. He had a personal "push" that is highly uncommon in lads of that age.

At the same time, he very much wanted feminine companionship. On June 22, he was introduced to a girl named "Maria".

"I should have escorted her home if she had not run away," he wrote. A July 29 entry says: "Casady says he is going to have some ice cream on the Fourth and I must get a girl." Ice cream was a rare luxury in Fort Des Moines. The diary doesn't say whether Hubbell got that date or not. Probably not. He was rather bashful. He went to a ball October 17 at the old Demoine House. He had a "splendid time but did not dance." He later joined a group taking dancing lessons. On another occasion, the diary says, Hubbell "broke a wishbone" with a girl. They "shook hands" after the bone was broken. He gleefully reports the wishbone incident in the diary but doesn't explain its significance.

In his leisure time, he played "chequers" and nearly always beat his opponents. He "mended my pants." He attended a temperance lecture. He "recited French" to himself and called on a "sick man at Lampson Sherman's house." (Lampson was a brother of Hoyt Sherman. Both Shermans were notable pioneer Des Moines residents.)

The diary reports that Hubbell bought himself a hat for 65 cents and a pair of pants for $2.75. He bought a lot in "Magnolia", presumably Magnolia, Iowa, from Casady for $25. The youth also made some progress socially. The Knights Templar lodge elected him chaplain. But he was restless. At the end of the 1855 diary, he wrote: "The old year has passed away and what a change it has wrought in me. How different are my circumstances and position from what it was one short year ago. Then I was living at home, aiming, striving, thinking, endeavoring to reach a different object and goal ... I have now about five months to stay with Casady and then what I shall do is uncertain. I have some idea of going to Sioux City. I hope for the best but am not prepared for the worst."

Hubbell also was still interested in getting into West Point. He talked about it with Marcellus M. Crocker, a Fort Des Moines attorney. Crocker, who later was one of Iowa's great Civil War generals, wrote a letter in Hubbell's behalf to U. S. Senator George W. Jones. But no West Point appointment materialized.

Meanwhile, Hubbell found out that he could get a job in Sioux City. He knew the Fort Des Moines land office job would end in a matter of months. There would be no need for a sizable land office after all the land had been claimed. The Sioux City land office would be open somewhat longer. He could work there and also earn some money recording deeds. He decided to go. He got his shoes soled and he bought a trunk. By this time, he had become acquainted with some of the girls of Fort Des Moines.

"Called on Kate Holland, Fanny Cooper, M. Tyler," he wrote in his diary. "Bid them goodbye." (This was the first mention of Fanny Cooper in his diary. She later became his wife.) On March 4, 1856, he boarded the stagecoach en route to Sioux City.

F. M. Hubbell at 16. From a daguerreotype taken in
Birmingham, Connecticut, in 1855.

3

Sioux City

SIOUX CITY TODAY is an hour's flight from Des Moines in a modern airliner. A century ago, the trip was a rugged affair that took 10 days in a stagecoach. There was no direct connection. Travelers had to go straight west to Council Bluffs, which took five days, and then north after a layover of two days. Sioux City was three days' journey north of Council Bluffs.

One stopover was at Ashton, a Monona County town that long since has vanished. Hubbell's coach reached Sioux City on a cold evening, March 13, 1856.

Sioux City was a tiny Missouri River outpost in the raw western wilderness. The population of whites was only 150. The Indians were everywhere. (One chief had the interesting name of "Smutty Bear.") Sioux City was less than two years old when Hubbell arrived. Dr. John K. Cook had laid out the townsite in 1854.

What happened to Hubbell the first six weeks of his Sioux City stay is not recorded. He evidently was too busy to pay any attention to his diary. The pages are blank. It is known, however, that he did go to work in the land office.

He resumed the diary April 21, 1856. On that day, he recorded in his own name a claim for 640 acres of land. Perhaps this was his first land venture in Woodbury County. He was still only 17 years old.

The Hubbell Sioux City diaries for 1856, 1857 and 1858 are notable for several reasons. For one thing, he wrote a line about the weather every day. He reported May 1, 1856, for example, as being "very cloudy, rained a little, very muddy." May 10 was "very pleasant" but May 12 was "cold and stormy." This may be the only day-by-day weather report available for the Sioux City area prior to August 1857.

Also, Hubbell loved the Missouri River steamboats. He faithfully recorded the comings and goings of the early steamboat traffic. His diaries are an authentic record of upper Missouri River steamboating in 1856 and 1857.

The steamboat was the best connection that Sioux City, Omaha and Council Bluffs had with the outside world in those days. The boats brought food, lumber, merchandise and equipment, all badly needed for the fast-growing civilization on the prairies. The steamboat also was a more comfortable way to travel than the bumpy stagecoach. The trouble was, the river didn't always run where you were going. In addition, there was no steamboat travel in the wintertime when the river was frozen over.

"The steamboat Gray Cloud went up this afternoon," Hubbell wrote April 21, 1856. He meant the boat departed upstream from Sioux City into the Dakotas. On May 2, he reported that "the Genoa arrived at dark." He went aboard the Genoa and "got my head shampooed." The Genoa barber, whoever he was, charged 15 cents for a shampoo.

On May 9, the diary says, "a ferry boat went over for the first time," from Sioux City to the South Dakota-Nebraska side of the river. June 2, 1856, was a big day in Missouri River history at Sioux City. That was the day the steamer Omaha arrived with a $70,000 cargo, all consigned to Sioux City. She had come a thousand miles up the river from St. Louis.

"She unloaded some of her goods before night," the Hubbell diary says. "The boys are getting drunk."

On June 17, the steamer Arabia was at the Sioux City wharf. On June 22, the Emma arrived, bringing home some Sioux City politicians from "the convention." (Presumably a political convention at Council Bluffs, or maybe Des Moines.)

The river boats also were instruments of pleasure. On July 1, 1857, the Omaha came down from Fort Randall, S. D.

"I attended a ball on her," Hubbell wrote. "I did not enjoy myself very much." He evidently wasn't much of a dancer at that time. "I cannot get loose so that my legs go off all right," he commented. "If I go to another (ball), I shall go with determination to do something or bust."

Boats were only part of his many interests in Sioux City. He also was absorbed in (1) speculation in property and in county obligations; (2) his studies, including law, and (3) girls.

Whatever happened to the 640 acres he claimed April 21, 1856, is not recorded in his diary. Perhaps he was too young to hold the land in his own name. On June 17, 1856, he took another claim.

"I had to induce father to come out and pre-empt (claim) it," Hubbell wrote. "I could not do so, being under 21 years of age." His father and his brother, Solon Hubbell, came out from Connecticut. They arrived in Sioux City July 6.

"Father and I went over to the claim and slept there, as it was necessary for us to live on the land," he wrote. "Mosquitoes are very thick. Could not sleep any. Had a rain in the night. Got wet."

Meanwhile, young Hubbell was busy recording property. On June 21, 1856, he finished recording the plat of Floyd City, an addition of Sioux City, "for which I received $6." Floyd City is largely occupied now by the Sioux City stockyards. On June 13, 1856, (while he still was 17) Hubbell bought five acres of land. On June 30, he obtained a city lot for $49.50.

On October 22, he "bought an interest" in the "town of Logan" and sold it immediately for $400. (He didn't record what he paid for it.) The same day he "bought an interest in Pacific City for 200 dollars." Less than a month later he sold that "interest" for $270, or a profit of $70.

By this time, he had decided to become a lawyer. He studied hard. But eight months after his arrival in Sioux City, he was homesick, not for Connecticut so much as for Fort Des Moines. He wrote: "I feel somewhat anxious to go to Fort Des Moines this winter and see some of the girls—I am very anxious to go. I think often how happy I shall be to meet my old acquaintances."

Before 1856 came to an end, he did go to Fort Des Moines on what he termed a "long visit." He really wanted to stay in Fort Des Moines. Phineas Casady, who was an attorney himself, promised to help him study law. Casady appears to have been rather slow about keeping the promise.

"Casady has not shown me anything yet," Hubbell complained in a diary entry for December 31, 1856. Then the boy wrote this long observation at the year's end: "I have labored during the past year exceeding hard and it has been a species of labor that is wearisome in the extreme; that of living in a new country, undergoing hardships and disadvantages of the same, constantly harassed with this one absorbing thought that if one should be sick or any other calamity befall him that he has no resources of his own, nor true and tried friends on whom he can rely for assistance in time of need. And yet I have passed through it all so far. I have done something for myself in a pecuniary point of view . . . Of infinitely greater importance is that I have secured for myself a good name and reputation which I esteem of more value than riches, and which no enemy can take from me."

He was proud of his record in Sioux City, except for two instances. With amazing candor, he wrote: "My course in general has been exemplary and in only two very trivial instances do I regret my conduct in the least, nor do I think reproach can attach to me for my conduct in the two cases above referred to; viz., the jumping of Weare's claim and the ferry license."

The diary does not explain what happened with regard to the Weare claim or the ferry license. Weare is the name of a Sioux City pioneer family.

"I have spent the past year very pleasantly considering my situation," Hubbell continued. "My property I think I can safely estimate at $4,000 and all paid for, which is very good beginning. My affections are not centered on anyone in particular. I am well pleased with Miss (Kate) Holland's appearance but she has some things about her which I consider faults; a want of proper and laudable anxiety to learn; however, this is very excusable as she is very young and I fear is not properly trained." (Hubbell wasn't 18 himself yet at the time he wrote this.)

"My standing here in Fort Des Moines is as good as I can wish," he added. "It seems to me that P. M. Casady, my friend and benefactor, does not do as much as is incumbent on him considering the letter he wrote to me before I started for his place in which he stated that he would have leisure time and would instruct me in the science of law, which he has not done yet."

Then Hubbell wrote this ultimatum: "If matters do not go to my satisfaction, which I sincerely hope they will, I shall return to Sioux City again."

His property interests in Sioux City were large for such a young fellow. At the end of the 1856 diary, he reported that he owned "an undivided interest of one half of 24 lots in Middle Sioux City, also one lot in Floyd City and an undivided one half of a lot in East Sioux City and 40 acres of land ... My lots numbering 13½ might be estimated at $240 each and my land at $20 an acre, which I think is not too high."

Much of Middle Sioux City is Sioux City business property now.

The diary demonstrates how much more valuable a dollar was in those days than it is now. Hubbell kept track in the back end of his 1856 diary of his income and expenses by months. In May of that year, his income was $17.35. His expenses totaled only $5.75. (He may have had a job where part of the pay was his board.) Most months, however, he took in more than that, and spent more. In June, he collected $78.88 and paid out $57.95. In July he received $77.05 and he paid out $65.30. These totals may have included his business dealings for those months. His board cost him $10 to $15 a month.

One day he found a dime on the floor of the land office. Meticulous person that he was, he recorded that 10 cents in his diary as a cash receipt for the day.

In January, 1857, he did a lot of thinking about whether to remain in Des Moines or to return to Sioux City. "My thought is much about my future course," he wrote. "Everything is well fixed at Sioux City but my desire to study law will overbalance my desire for wealth."

Casady finally advised him to return to Sioux City, and he did so. He left Des Moines February 20, 1857. In some ways, he was loath to go. His dancing lessons were happy occasions. ("I have felt a little dizzy from the dancing," he wrote one night.) Also, Kate Holland had had quite an effect on him. Two days before he left for Sioux City, the youth wrote: "My emotions are these: Heretofore I have been disposed to love Kate Holland but am now disinclined, although I have strange feelings when I meet her but she is not sensible, educated or accomplished and knows but little of any kind of work."

4

Mary Wilkins

A STUDY OF the Hubbell diaries has brought to light for the first time a poignant little love story that is nearly 100 years old.

Mary Wilkins was Sioux City's first school teacher. She arrived April 24, 1857, on the steamer Omaha. Her home was in Keosauqua, Iowa. Elsewhere, Mary has been described as a brunette with "flashing eyes and a vivacious manner." She was 20 years old at the time.

Fred Hubbell was 18 when he became acquainted with Mary. He was a hard-working young man who already had gained a reputation in Sioux City for being somewhat of a genius in making money. His associates would have been astonished had they known that inwardly he also was a lonely and rather senti· mental person.

"Was introduced to Miss Wilkins and went around town with her shopping," Hubbell wrote April 29. He underlined that sentence in his diary. He appears to have been smitten immediately.

23

The affair progressed slowly at first. Mary was not mentioned again until July 13, when Hubbell "called on the school ma'am and had a good confidential conversation with her." That visit did not alleviate a spell of homesickness that he had over a period of several weeks. On July 27, he wrote, he "took a walk by moonlight and thought of the dear ones far away." August 1, he again walked in the moonlight. "I thought of home and of the pleasure I would enjoy if I could only be there now. But I must bide my time and hope that all will be well."

On August 20, he wrote: "Read some light reading this evening until late. I yearn for something to love and hope I may find it." Two days later he wrote this soul-searching statement: "I feel there is a void in my heart, that I am passing through the world without any object in view, with nothing to love. With something to live (for), all my latent energies would be called forth . . . I would then have something to live for."

His thoughts were not centered on Mary Wilkins altogether. He called on a Mattie Jamison with regularity. He took her to at least one dance. He was not enthralled by her. He much preferred Mary. On September 10, he again "called on the school marm this eve after school was out."

"I think I could make an impression without much effort," Hubbell wistfully wrote, then added in a boy's elaborate language: "I have a notion to try Miss Wilkins and see if her feelings are consonant with mine." But his hopes evidently were not high. The next day he wrote this comment: "I would give anything if I knew of a woman that I could love. It would do my soul good to have some worthy object on whom to bestow my warmest affections. I hope I shall soon see her if she is yet in being."

His desire for companionship again was demonstrated September 14, when the steamer E. A. Ogden docked at noon. "Went up to the boat and saw some of the dancing but did not participate," he wrote. On September 21, he confessed: "Felt rather sentimental all day. Am almost decided to fall in love with the first woman I see who is not married."

There was no church on Sunday, September 27. "I have felt more lonesome today than I have for a long time before," he wrote. "Took a short walk upon the hill and then went up Perry Creek and got some plums."

Hubbell visited Mary the next day and "had a pleasant chat with her." The name of Fanny Cooper back in Des Moines, Fred's future wife, crept into the diary at this point. It may be that Fanny and Fred had some sort of an understanding that is not recorded in the diary. At any rate, in discussing Mary, Hubbell wrote: "I could learn to love her without much trouble. In fact, I like her pretty well even now, but the thoughts of little Fanny Cooper dispel all ideas of matrimony until I have asked her consent. I hope to see her soon and see if she suits me well enough." He did not say what "consent" he needed from Fanny.

He was depressed again October 3. "I feel lonely today," he wrote. "No one has been here yet and everything looks so dismal and gloomy. It rains this evening and I have done nothing but think of the future and wish and hope for I scarce know what, but I am not happy. . . . Surely I am enjoying the stern realities of this life with more pain than pleasure."

Getting a letter made a tremendous difference. Fred was dispirited again October 6, "but since I got the letters I am a little better pleased with the world." He had gotten three letters that day, two from relatives.

On December 18, he had a date with Mattie Jamison. He succeeded in kissing her and he. exultantly reports that fact in his diary. But his real interest still was Mary. On December 20, he took her to church.

"She is very affectionate and I believe I have made an impression and I am quite sure she has made an impression on me," he wrote. "I wish that she was 3 or 4 years younger and then I would engage her services for life, the labor to commence 2 or 3 years hence."

He believed himself too young for marriage. And he didn't like the idea of Mary being older than he was. A week later, he wrote: "I am of the opinion that Mary is a pretty good girl and would make a first rate wife." Then he added: "I think some of fooling her by making her think I am going away and so have a scene when we part when I will try to get a few tender words from her and a few sweet kisses."

On December 27, he took her to church and asked her if she were engaged. "She said no and that her age was 20½," the diary relates. (Fred was nearly 19 by this time.) "I told her I thought of going away Tuesday. She gave me a ring for a Christmas gift and I had a long and interesting conversation about matrimony with her. . . . We then shook hands and as I held her hand in mine I said shall I have one kiss? She hesitated only an instant and then gave it. I am almost in love and wish I was 23 and then I would propose."

Romance was progressing by January 6, 1858. They decided to read Latin together! "Called on Mary this evening," he wrote. "We had a long, interesting and to me a very pleasant conversation. She proposed to read Virgil together, to which proposition I assented. I remained until after 9 o'clock and then tore myself away."

On January 18, he "went up and read Virgil with Mary and had a good long talk with her. I think I can kiss her after two or three more visits. I will try, at all events. She has more good solid sense than any girl I ever saw, but she is too old for me, or I am too young for her."

All the while he kept trying to determine whether he had any chance with her. On January 25, he wrote: "I put questions very plain and ascertained that she thinks, or professes to think, that she is too old and that I am impressible. But I will show her that I can exist without her and too that I am not impressible either. I feel relieved of quite a load and can enter into the spirit of the contest with zeal."

On February 3, he untruthfully insisted: "There is no soft spot in my heart yet." Five nights later, they again studied Latin together. The crucial time had come.

"When the lesson was over we conversed and in the conversation I told her that I loved her," the diary says. "She said that she reciprocates but I told her to think of it until she saw me again and then tell me how much she loved me. My mind is already made up that I love her dearly."

On February 14, Valentine's day, he "kissed her and pledged my love and she to me, something I have never done before, probably shall never again." Fred was deeply moved February 18. On that day he told Mary the "one great secret of my life," the ailment of his mother. He did not say what was the matter with his mother. It may have been cancer. Mary was not repelled. With a touch of reverence, he wrote: "She still says she loves me and will always do so and if I am overtaken in the prime of manhood by that awful complaint that she will take care of me. Oh, how much I love her for that. Her love and her fineness will be enough to stimulate me to high and noble deeds. While my health remains to me, she shall never be ashamed of my conduct or regret that she has bestowed her love on me."

On February 20, he wrote that "I am scarcely happy except when with her which is pretty often lately and I believe she enjoys my society as well as I do hers." He was concerned the next day lest he was not paying sufficient attention to business. After a tryst with Mary he reported: "She seemed sorry when I had to go. I may not have seemed so to her but it was there. I felt I must now attend to business closely . . . so that when I am of age I shall be ready to marry. The time will pass quickly and two years will try our loves. For my own part, I have no fears for the result but Mary fears even if she does not doubt."

The first hint that all was not well for Fred came a few days later. Mary told him she was not going to a dance. She nevertheless went, and not with him. "She was very sorry and we kissed and forgave each other," he wrote afterwards. "It was one of the most pleasant evenings I have ever spent with her. I know that she sincerely regrets going and that she loves me . . . " He resolved to "exert all my energy now to prepare myself to make her happy and I trust that I shall succeed. It seems as though the future might be happy to us."

On February 27 occurred what proved to be an ominous development. Fred called on Mary. While he was there, a group of visitors came in. Among them was Charles B. Rustin. Rustin was an energetic young fellow around Sioux City. He and Hubbell sometimes were partners in speculative ventures. Rustin, too, had his eye on Mary. But Fred was not aware of the dangers ahead to his cause. He was so sure everything was all right that he told Mary March 10, he could not read Virgil with her any more. The diary doesn't say why. Perhaps he decided he had better work harder in order to get ready for marriage two years hence.

There seems to have been a touch of mischief about Mary. The March 16 diary entry says: "Have read the Reveries of a Bachelor which Mary gave to me to peruse. They are very good and some are something like mine."

The diary at this point disclosed the fact that Fred had no monopoly on Mary's time anyway. On March 22, he wrote: "Field takes Mary to a party at Townsend's tonight. I was not invited, bad luck to them. This makes two parties at that place and I have not been invited." (The "Field" whom Hubbell mentions may have been Joseph Field, brother of Marshall

Letter of application written by F. M. HUBBELL
while at Sioux City in 1857.

Part of the early Hubbell diary is in shorthand. This July 10, 1858 page says: *"Read 40 pages and left off at page No. 350. Called on Mary at noon and she made some excuses and wanted me to call tonight which I did, finally reconciled myself to the matter, and she promised never to let anything of that kind ever happen again. I embraced her and then departed. Bought 200 dollars worth of County Orders of Doct. Cook and I think Rustin will want to sell. If he does, I shall buy them."*

Field of Chicago. Joe Field lived in Sioux City in the late 1850's.)

So far as Fred could tell, he still rated No. 1 with Mary. He saw her April 13, and "had a few kisses." He visited Miss Jamison a couple of times, but Mary was still foremost.

"Mary, the future happiness and prospect, occupies my mind in all its leisure hours," he wrote April 21. "Time is the only barrier which I can not overcome, except by itself."

But time was running out. On June 16, he wrote somberly: "Saw Charley Rustin and with my Mary." On June 20, he added this unhappy comment: "Oh, I must not be disappointed in this of all things earthly the dearest to me."

On June 23, Fred was indignant. He wrote: "I am under the impression that Mary will go to Dakota with Charley Rustin or someone else and if she (does) I shall call her to account because she has told me two or three times that she would not go. If she had not positively refused to go, I should have asked her myself but on account of her refusal I did not ask."

He met Mary on the street next day and asked if she were going. "She said it depended upon circumstances," the diary reports. "I believe she will go and if she does it will not have a tendency to increase my sum of happiness. Time will determine."

To his chagrin, she went. The next day he wrote: "She has gone and I am surprised, disappointed, grieved and almost angry to think that she would go with Field after saying so positively and emphatically that she would not go at all. She is just like all the balance of the girls. They can not see far enough to discern the consequences and effects of their own acts."

On June 25, he was "sick at heart."

"I can not conceive any reason for Mary's conduct and if I can not get a good explanation then the (relationship) with her that has given me so much happiness shall be at an end," he wrote, then added bravely: "I have a heart which no woman, and much less one that professes to love me, shall trifle with. Tomorrow evening, hoping to find her alone, I will go and try and see if I can feel happy again in her society."

Alas for Fred! When he reached her home, he found that Mary had gone walking with Rustin. Hubbell met them on his way home. "I stopped a moment," the diary records, "and looked at her with a gaze which if it revealed my real feeling must have caused one pang of sorrow at least to her . . . I am miserable tonight but it shall soon be at an end. If she is worthy of me, I shall soon know it and if not I am rescued from a fate worse than death. I am resolved not to call again to see her for two weeks and this resolution I will strive to keep religiously and I never failed yet."

In this instance, his resolution was not strong enough. After seeing Mary in church, he wrote: "I love her better than life itself and there is not a waking hour in which I do not think of her."

The next day he "had a little talk" with Mary. "She does not appear to think there is anything wrong," he wrote sadly. On June 29, he found out that Mary had gone riding with Rustin.

"I must see her and know. whether she will marry next spring or not," Fred decided. She told him the next day. "She says she does not want to marry within 8 months from now," he reported. "She has heretofore expressed her willingness to embark whenever I am ready but now she has changed her mind . . . "

Fred refused to recognize defeat. On July 19, he saw her at the schoolhouse. "She may not have changed in heart," he wrote, "but in manners and actions she has certainly. I am now on my guard and if I see anything that indicates a growing coldness on her part I shall not fail to remember it." The coldness was already there but he was hopelessly blind to it.

On July 24, he expressed a wish that she would go away "for I want to see what letters she will write, and how often." (Whether she would have written any at all is highly doubtful.) On July 26, he saw her out horseback riding with Rustin. But still Fred refused to give up. There is this thread of desperation in the diary for July 27, 1858: "Have thought a great deal about Mary for the last few days and I know that I love her with an affection pure, noble and unchangeable. On account of my youth, I think she fears to trust me. I know not how to reassure her and allay her fears but truth, honesty, kindness and my whole heart she has and will have them all. Oh, how I wish I could unburden my whole heart to her and she to me. She wishes that I would not ask for so many kisses and caresses as she thinks it wrong . . . "

His hopes soared again July 30. He said: " . . . She says she will appoint a time for our union before she goes away and I am very glad of it, for I know just what to expect." But his spirits were dampened again August 7, when he went to see Mary. The inevitable Rustin was there.

"I have not as much confidence in Mary as I once had," Fred mourned. "I believe that she encouraged Field and Rustin or they would not be there so much. She has only four weeks and two days to keep school and . . . I shall be glad, for her letters will assist me in judging her real sentiments concerning me."

The next day he was hurt when he came into an office where she was writing. "She paid little attention," he wrote, "and did not seem to care whether I stayed or not and I therefore took occasion to leave quite soon."

There was a ball aboard the riverboat Rowena August 16. Mary told Fred she had promised to go with Field. She went walking with Rustin instead. Wrote the unhappy Hubbell: "One thing is very certain and that is that she does not think as much of my society as she did three months ago."

He still refused to face the fact. On August 19, he commented: "I think I should be content if I knew what Mary was going to do with my future prospects. I had rather she would say no at once than keep me in this everlasting suspense, but such is the way of true love."

The next day the lonely young man wrote: "Times pass rather heavily. I long for love again. I was happy once but now I feel that she can be no more to me. But the hours will soon speed by when I shall hear from her own lips how near our destinies are united. How happy a moment it would be to me when I could call her wife."

The blow descended August 22, when Fred went to Mary's house to get her to go to Bible class. She didn't want to go. "I had a little talk with her and she now wants to take back all that she has said," the diary discloses. "So we have concluded to quit. It has terminated just as I have long expected and now I am alone in the world again. Oh how happy I might have been but she now loves Rustin, of this I am convinced. I hope he will make her happy. It is of no use to cry now for what is lost to me forever. She made me promise that I would never tell anyone of what has happened of which I will keep sacred as I have all the other promises I made to her."

He never did tell either. The secret was kept from that day until this.

On August 23, at the schoolhouse, Mary told Fred that she had exchanged engagement rings with Rustin. The grief-stricken Hubbell wrote: "I blame myself for most of it . . . and must acknowledge that we are perhaps not fitted for each other though I could have lived happy with her."

The next day he again sought solace by writing in his diary. "I can not blame Mary for her course except for not telling me sooner," he observed. "I have learned something and experienced a great deal of happiness with her and it is all over and I must begin again. I could have been happy with her but I fear she would not have been contented."

Fred couldn't stay away from Mary no matter how much it hurt him. On August 25, he again stopped to see her. Rustin came in "and I left them to themselves." "Oh, how happy he must be with her," Fred wrote. "She looked more lovely than ever to me but I am resigned and we are friends which is all I can expect. I must get her to give me some advice which she says she will do." If the advice ever was given, Hubbell did not make a record of it in his diary.

The heavy-hearted Hubbell gave Mary a translation of Virgil September 7. "Called on her tonight and found her alone," he wrote. "She sang and played to me and we conversed until 10 o'clock. . . . She thinks I am an egotist but I convinced her that I was not as much of one as I might lead her to think. We parted to meet perhaps never. . . ."

The Sioux City diaries of Frederick M. Hubbell come to an end at the close of 1858. In fact, there are no annual diaries from 1858 until 1881. Whether they were lost, or whether he did not keep them, is not known.

Mary Wilkins and Charles B. Rustin were married, probably in 1859.

Fred Hubbell. never mentioned Mary again. He returned to Des Moines to take up permanent residence in 1861. In 1863 he married Fanny Cooper.

5

Hard Times

TO SAY THAT Fred Hubbell spent all his time and thoughts brooding over Mary Wilkins in 1857 and 1858 would be quite erroneous. The diaries show that he was deeply occupied with Sioux City's government and business affairs, and with his own speculations.

He had one job in the land office and another in the recorder's office. He was also deputy clerk of the District Court. Since the clerk never was present, he did the clerk's work—and collected his fees.

"Made out naturalization papers for a Frenchman and German for $1.50 each," he wrote March 16, 1857. "Took acknowledgments and made an American out of a foreigner." He also made out the Woodbury County tax lists.

Besides his official duties, Hubbell was always lending and borrowing money. He bought and sold a large volume of county warrants. He spent considerable time studying law, logic and shorthand. And he did all he could to help a Sioux City attorney overcome alcoholism.

Even on those occasions when Fred felt sentimental, he did not limit his diary comments to Mary Wilkins. For example, on April 21, 1858, he wrote: "Had dinner early and supper late. Made up the records before dark. Mary, the future happiness and prospect, occupies my mind in all its leisure hours. It looks very much like a thunderstorm this evening. My lumber for fencing came today."

He really didn't have much time for moping. There was a depression in 1857. Times were hard. Hard times were important to Hubbell for two reasons. First he had to take care lest he himself be wiped out. Then, he looked upon a depression as a time of opportunity. He knew that periods of extremely low prices would not last. Thus, he usually was willing to invest heavily in properties in times of depressions. That is one of the reasons why he was able to build up such a sizable fortune during his lifetime.

At the same time, the downward trend in 1857 worried 18-year-old Fred. On September 24, of that year, he wrote: "I am much oppressed at the tight times and am afraid it is going to injure my fortunes not a little. I have a strong heart and can commence the world anew if it must be so, and I should not be at all surprised if it should happen. The steamer Omaha arrived today with not much freight."

On October 3, he really was blue. He wrote: "The prospect this winter is chilling indeed with no employment and still less money to pay my expenses and then I am in debt which is worse than all the rest."

He did not explain what he meant by "no employment." He probably was out of a job temporarily. There was a period when the job of recording deeds was taken from him. Also, District Court work may have been light, or non-existent, at the time. On October 29, he reported earning 50 cents for the day.

"Hard times, come no more," he said in his diary. He was determined that he should not let a day pass without taking in some money. "I hope I shall sell these laths and nails tomorrow so as to do something each day," he wrote October 23. Those old "poorhouse" thoughts seemed to bother him. On November 18, he said: "I want to go to Des Moines but do not want to lose money in the operation. If I stay here I shall pay nothing for board and (stove) wood and will save a little money as fees (clerk of court). If I go, I shall spend more than $100 . . . I hope to be able to get $100 fees during the next two or three months . . . I want to make enough money to get out of debt and then I do not care."

By December 4, however, he wasn't in such bad financial condition. He had "on hand $140 in gold and over $65 in paper." At the end of the 1857 diary, he wrote: "The old year is dead. I am not much better off than I was one year ago, except in experience which has been a dear school to me as well as others."

The depression hit the county government of Woodbury County. The county treasury was virtually empty. County warrants sank far below par in value. Hubbell saw his chance. He bought up as many warrants as he could finance . . . On January 2, 1858, he reported: "Bought a county warrant of W. M. Crawford of $13 and paid him $4 for it." On January 5, he "bought $290.50 of county warrants and paid $74.25. I have now bought $379 of them at 26¼c on the dollar. I think that is trading pretty well."

On March 6, he paid one John Braden $80 for a $300 warrant. On April 26, he said he was "about out of money but shall keep on buying orders as long as I have a cent." On June 19, he said he had $1,200 in warrants, "which will do pretty well for a young man who wants to get married." (This was during the Mary Wilkins era.)

He used the warrants to pay back taxes on delinquent real estate. Then he apparently sold the real estate and used the cash to buy more warrants. His system worked. The depression was easing. Conditions were on the mend and before the end of 1858 Woodbury warrants were worth 50 cents on the dollar. Hubbell more than doubled his money on some of the warrants.

Fred abandoned the land business completely for a time and concentrated on warrants. On April 30, 1858, he wrote: "I have made up my mind in view of the tight times and the fact that there is so much land coming in to the market in Nebraska this fall that times will be dull in this neck of the woods and that more money will be made in paying taxes than in locating lands. I am on the inside track of this county and by a little effort can keep up without trouble."

By November 15, his finances seemed to be good again. On that date, he balanced his individual account books and "find that my profit and loss shows an increase of about $574, without taking into account the profits on county orders. I commence my books anew and hope to do still better next year."

In addition, he was in partnership with Rustin on some speculations. That partnership apparently showed $275 profit for the year. (The fact that Rustin had taken Mary Wilkins away from him did not seem to bother Hubbell at all businesswise.)

On December 4, Hubbell's outlook was so much better that he wrote: "I thank my Creator for the many blessings that he bestows upon me, unmerited as they are."

The improvement in the market on county warrants was not the only reason for Fred's brightened outlook. On July 30, he had got the job of preparing the county tax list. That task gave him a steady income of $1 a day. That pay doesn't sound like much now. But that daily dollar was mighty comforting in 1858.

Characteristically, he was always on the watch for additional ways to make money. Northwest Iowa counties were in the process of becoming organized for the first time in those years. On October 10, Hubbell wrote: "I have a new prospect. It is that I sell the newly organized counties their books and get the contracts of posting all of their books up to date and make out the list of the lands to be taxed." He may have had some success with that venture.

This Sioux City period was important in Hubbell's life for reasons other than money. He platted much of the property in fast-growing Sioux City. (The town had a population of 150 when he arrived in 1856 and probably 2,500 by late 1858.) That gave him wonderful experience for his later massive real estate operations in Des Moines.

As was the case in Des Moines (or wherever he happened to be), Hubbell studied continuously while in Sioux City. His daily diary often carries such reports as this: "Read 100 lines of Virgil." He also studied Pitman shorthand (and wrote some of his diary in that script.)

More vital, however, was his study of law. Day after day, night after night, he read the lawbooks. On August 11, 1857, for example, he wrote: "Very hot day. Finished Blackstone and read 40 pages of Kent." He spent long hours reading "Greenleaf on Evidence."

Blackstone, Kent and Greenleaf are famous early legal authorities.

On April 24, 1858, he was admitted to the practice of law. The Sioux City Eagle, local weekly newspaper, carried a story about it. The newspaper commented: "Mr. Hubbell is a young man of good abilities and possesses those qualities which will insure success. Our best wishes attend him." He was 19 years old at the time.

One interesting side in Hubbell's Sioux City life was his concern over a lawyer named "Currier." Fred liked Currier and enjoyed talking with him about experiences in the practice of frontier law. In addition, Currier was "disposed to assist" the youth in the study of law. But Currier liked his liquor too well. On November 6, 1857, Hubbell wrote: "Currier commenced drinking today and was drunk all day long. I regret it exceedingly but it can not be avoided now. I shall try tomorrow and see if I can do anything to keep him straight . . . He has such an appetite that he can not resist the temptation. He says he will stop and I hope and pray that he will . . ."

The November 8 report was: "Snowed almost all day. Currier still keeps drunk . . ." The next day, young Hubbell "stayed with Currier some. He is pretty drunk although he attended to some business this forenoon . . . I believe I have more interest in his welfare than in anyone else in town."

A few days later, Fred again took Currier in tow.
"I got him to come down here," the diary said. "I also
got him a bottle of brandy and have dealt out small
doses to him. I am going to try to get him straight
again . . . Gave Currier some morphine tonight."

Fred spent most of the next day waiting on Currier. "I think he will reform and come to something
yet," Hubbell wrote. "He has now gone to bed and
is asleep upon some morphine . . . I shall make a grand
effort. I watered his brandy and threw half of it away.
He is almost delirious tonight."

They had quite a time with Currier November 16.
Hubbell played a game of billiards with him in an
effort to keep him sober. Then Fred took the attorney
to the old Sioux City House to spend the night.

"He (Currier) took opium and was nearly crazy
and I got up and called J. P. Flagg and they slept together the balance of the night," the diary says. "Currier fell downstairs once during the night."

After Currier got up one night to drink gin, Hubbell commented: "It will not do to trust a man that
gets drunk with any secrets. I have told him too many
and will put a stop to it."

On January 1, 1858, New Year's Day, Hubbell
"followed Currier around some but concluded it would
do no good. I am resolved that I will not touch ardent
spirits in any manner unless I am sick." With a very

few exceptions, he followed that rule all his life. Only on the rarest of occasions did he take a drink.

Hubbell did not concern himself much with Currier's problem after that. It may be that the lawyer succeeded in overcoming his difficulty. Currier's name appears a few times in the 1858 diary in connection with business deals around Sioux City. Hubbell made no further mention of Currier's troubles with liquor.

Speaking of business, the diary carries some revealing facts on interest rates in pioneer Iowa, and particularly around Sioux City. Today, interest charges usually are 5 or 6 per cent, and often less. In 1857, Hubbell thought he would be nice to Aunt Caroline back in Connecticut. He wrote her a letter and "told her to send money if she wanted 40% for it and I would give her a note to that amount." She sent him $210.

He was to regret that loan later. In March of 1858 Fred expressed a wish that "I did not owe her (Caroline) anything but if I have good luck I will be all right in a year." He finally sold Woodbury County warrants at 50 cents on the dollar late in 1858 in a determined campaign to get her paid off. He probably succeeded but the diary does not say.

Fred inserted warnings to himself in with his reports of day-by-day happenings in Sioux City. On August 11, 1857, he wrote this rambling entry in his

PHINEAS M. CASADY, who gave F. M. Hubbell his first
job in Fort Des Moines.

Marcellus M. Crocker, Civil War general who was a member of the law firm with which Hubbell became associated in 1861.

diary: "Very hot day. Heard of the murder of Fitz-patrick and went over to see about it . . . I must try to get the good will of everyone more than I do and co-incide in their views and cling to my own opinions with less pertinacity even if I know I am right. Flat-tery will affect every man to a certain extent which is a maxim as true as it is general . . ."

He had considerable confidence in himself busi-nesswise. On January 1, 1858, right before his 19th birthday, he wrote: "I can not complain. I have made some mistakes but can look around and see many who have made more serious ones than I have myself. Who at the same time bear a reputation of being the shrewd-est businessmen in town. My own self-confidence has been increasing for the past six months until now I would not trust another's judgment as soon as my own in most matters."

On January 8, 1858, he commented: "I find that people here are willing to give me credit for all that is due me. They consult my views and my opinions and observe my remarks and follow my instructions which I may give. There is one thing to fear and that is I may gain too much confidence in myself so that I may be overbearing and not conservative. I will try to guard against it."

He felt that he rated well in the Sioux City com-munity. On January 28, 1858, he wrote: "I believe I am on good terms with almost anyone in town and if

I was 21 I could easily be elected to any office in the county next October but infants are nix."

He wasn't at all certain that he wanted to remain in Sioux City and he didn't in the end. He wanted to return to Des Moines to practice law. As early as November 12, 1857, before the 18-year-old Fred was admitted to the bar, he wrote this letter to Casady & Crocker, Des Moines law firm: "I requested McCall when he was here last to speak to you and see if I could get a situation with you during the coming winter and perhaps for two or three years to come if I can arrange my business at this place. If I come this winter I want to earn my expenses. Can I be of that advantage to you? I have read Blackstone and Kent through *hurriedly* this summer . . . Please write to me soon and let me know what the prospect is . . ."

The prospects evidently were not encouraging at the moment. Hubbell was not successful in making that connection in Des Moines until 1861.

In the intervening years, he and some other young fellows went up north of Sioux City and founded a brand new Iowa county.

The closing pages of the Sioux City diaries carry a touch of the informality of life in such a pioneer town. For example, Hubbell did not go home one night because of a heavy rain. He stayed in another individual's office. Fred regretted his decision.

"Slept four in a bed," he complained. "I shall not sleep there again unless the weather is so bad that I cannot get home."

6

22 Important Years

IN THE LATE fall of 1859, Fred Hubbell and several companions left Sioux City with a team of horses, a wagon and camping equipment.

They rolled northward over the rough and frozen trail into new country. They were on their way to set up a county government in Sioux County, Iowa. Their purpose in organizing such a government was simple and elemental: They were out to make some money if possible.

There is little Hubbell diary record of this project. The annual diaries are missing for 22 consecutive years after 1858. He may not have kept the diaries, or they may have been lost. Those 22 years are vital in the Hubbell history. It was then that he began to accumulate large blocks of real estate, to build railroads. It was then that he brought together the forces which started the Equitable. That also was the period when the B. F. Allen bankruptcy shook the whole middle-west.

Available in the Hubbell papers are a few news-

paper clippings of the period. And a sketchy "perpetual" diary provides a little information.

The "perpetual" diary is a large blank-page book.
Hubbell wrote all the dates of the year at the tops of
365 pages. For example, one page is headed "January
3." Under that date, he recorded various year-by-year
happenings in this fashion:

"1904—$1,000 insurance Asbury ME church ex-
pires today."

"1921—Coliseum lease with free rental expired
January 1."

"1916—Grenville M. Dodge died today. Was born
April 12, 1831. 84 years, 8 months, 22 days."

The "perpetual" diary contains widely varied frag-
ments of information. Under April 2, 1886, he wrote:
"Clean cisterns and tanks." Under March 7, 1892, the
entry is: "Started to go around the world today with
O. H. Perkins." October 4, 1885: "First frost this
morning." He faithfully recorded the deaths of all of
his contemporaries, such as the October 3, 1913, entry:
"Chester C. Cole died today, 89 years, 3 months, 29
days." Most of the time covered in the "perpetual"
diary also is taken care of in the annual diaries. Thus,
he kept two diaries some of the time.

There are at least three entries dealing with the
Sioux County adventure in the "perpetual" diary. He
did not have that diary with him at that time. The
entries obviously were written many years afterwards.

Under date of December 9, 1859, the diary says: "As I remember it, FMH and 3 others landed in Sioux County about today. The others were Joseph Bell, William H. Frame and Emerson Stone to organize Sioux County."

Phineas Casady in Des Moines encouraged Hubbell to go into the unorganized northwest Iowa territory and "start something." Casady said: "There is a whole county just waiting as nature made it, waiting for civilization." Hubbell recalled later that he "took the cue and with three other wide awake young fellows" moved northward.

Casady was not the only source of inspiration. Roistering trappers around the streets and bars of Sioux City long had told stories of the fertile and beautiful wilderness to the north. Hubbell and his associates heard those stories and talked over the possibilities of establishing there.

The "Historical Atlas of Iowa," published in 1875, says: "Among the earliest white settlers of Sioux County were F. M. Hubble, E. L. Stone, Joseph Bell, W. H. Frame and Francis Frame. They located in the valley of the Big Sioux prior to 1860, while the county was organized that same season . . . The election was held at a place known as 'Buzzard's Roost'."

"F. M. Hubble" and Frederick M. Hubbell were one and the same person. Hubbell does not list a "Francis Frame" in the party.

The four young men excavated a dugout in the side of a ravine near the Big Sioux. They cut timbers in the ravine to support the roof and walls. This dugout evidently was "Buzzard's Roost." They dug another hillside hole for the horses. The location is about three miles south of the present town of Hawarden.

Dyke's "Story of Sioux County" says the four were the only white men living in the county at the time. That might well have been the case. This was a period of Indian massacres. For years afterward, there was no general migration of white families into Sioux County. Fear of Indian depredations was one reason. The Civil War also may have slowed the westward movement of families.

Headquarters established, Hubbell and Bell walked all the way back to Sioux City. They started the journey January 17, 1860, Hubbell's 21st birthday. That trip on foot covered more than 40 miles. Purpose of the trip was to petition the authorities in Sioux City for power to organize the new county. The Sioux County area then was attached to Woodbury County for taxation and judicial purposes. Permission was granted.

Hubbell and Bell returned to the dugout armed with official papers. Sioux County's first election was held the following month. Hubbell's recollection was that the date was Feb. 7, 1860. Dyke says only four votes were cast. The candidates all voted for each other.

There is some dispute over who was elected to what office. Hubbell wrote that he was elected Clerk of the District Court; Bell, County Judge; Stone, County Treasurer, and Frame, Sheriff. The "Atlas" says Frame was elected judge, not Bell.

There is no conflict, however, over the fact that Hubbell was elected clerk. This was the only time in his life he ever was elected to public office. It was the only time he ever was a candidate.

The dugout became the Sioux County "courthouse." The county officers had no settlers to tax. Nevertheless, the officers were entitled under the law to draw salaries. They took care of this by issuing warrants which they sold, probably in Sioux City. There was nothing wrong in this. Other counties down through the years had gotten started the same way. Somebody had to organize county governments.

The officers spent a pleasant late winter and spring. They brought along plenty of provisions. Hunting and fishing were good. They read, played cards, played the fiddle. Hubbell was the cook. The winter was cold and the wolves were numerous. Hubbell's companions called his cookery "wolf bait."

In the spring, the officers established a townsite on 120 acres of nearby land. They voted bonds to build a new courthouse. There is no record of how large the bond issue was. They built a log courthouse 1½ stories high. The workmanship on the building is said to have been excellent.

It appears that the officers, who still constituted the entire white population of the county, both lived and officially functioned in that courthouse. The building had portholes for use in fighting off warlike Indians, or white marauders. Apparently none came.

The county officers agreed to name the new county seat town "Calliope." Hubbell provided the name. He once heard a steam calliope on a Missouri River boat. He liked calliope music.

Two of the officers liked to spend much of their time hanging around the bars in Sioux City. Hubbell and Stone were described by Dyke, however, as "clear-headed young businessmen" to whom an "idling and carousing life (was not) agreeable to their taste or sense of honor." They rarely went to Sioux City.

After about 18 months, Hubbell and Stone sold their interest in the county to two young men named Lewis and Murray. The price is not known. One theory is that Hubbell and Stone received $3,000.

It has been said that Hubbell and Stone left the county only $3,000 in debt. The officers, however, had built the courthouse and had constructed bridges across Dry Creek and Six-Mile Creek. In addition, the four had drawn county officer salaries for a year and a half.

These are the reasons why some authorities believe the $3,000 estimate is too low.

Dyke quotes Hubbell as saying he had $700 in warrants in his possession when he left Calliope. Hubbell reported that he lost those warrants through the bankruptcy of a friend to whom he had entrusted them.

The name "Calliope" long since has disappeared from the Iowa map. The town was county seat until 1872 when the county government was taken to Orange City, where it remains to this day.

Hubbell left Sioux County in 1861. He paused briefly in Sioux City and then came to Des Moines where he lived the rest of his life.

There is no information available about Hubbell in connection with the Civil War. He did not go into service. It was not that he was afraid of military life. He had tried in vain in the 1850's to get into West Point. He was not drafted for the Union army. As a matter of record only about 50 men were drafted from Polk County all during the war. The county came very nearly meeting its complete quota through voluntary enlistments.

Hubbell was not criticized in the Des Moines newspapers of the Civil War period. The newspapers were not gentle in those days, especially when talking about Democrats. And Hubbell was a Democrat. He must have had some good reason for remaining at home.

On June 1, 1861, he got a job as a law clerk in the office of Jefferson S. Polk and Phineas Casady, leading Des Moines lawyers. But Hubbell was destined not to remain a clerk long. As a result of his Sioux County venture, he was not broke. At least, he had quite a little money by January 1, 1862. The "perpetual diary" for that date says: "I was admitted to partnership today with P. M. Casady and J. S. Polk. I pay $1,200 for one-third of library and one-third of office furniture."

Casady withdrew from the firm in 1865. Polk and Hubbell continued to operate together as a law firm until 1887.

Hubbell may well have laid the base for his fortune in the early 1860's. Des Moines had a population of 3,965 in 1860. By 1870, the population had increased to 12,035, or more than threefold. And by 1880 it was 22,408.

A good way to get rich in those days (or any day) was to acquire considerable property in a town just before it gained a lot of population. Hubbell undoubtedly bought a lot of property before the first railroad reached Des Moines in 1866 (from Keokuk). Railroads were a strong stimulant to a town's prosperity in those days. There were six railroads serving Des Moines by 1875.

This was the time when he decided to emphasize investment in downtown real estate. In later years, he used to advise: "Have all your earnings in one place where you can see it in one afternoon. I hated to walk so I never bought anything that took me longer than 15 minutes from the office to inspect."

It may have been in the Civil War period (or shortly after) that Hubbell bought the land now known as "Factory Addition" immediately south of downtown Des Moines. This industrial tract stretches south to the Raccoon River. Says one authority: "Prior to 1890, F. M. Hubbell acquired a large tract of land lying south of the railroad tracks which came to be known as the 'Factory district.' It was low land, subject to overflow from the Raccoon River, but if protected, was an ideal location for industries requiring transportation facilities; and it was within a reasonable distance of the business district. Beginning in about 1890, and continuing for many years thereafter, the Hubbell interests . . . began the development of this Factory district by protecting it from overflow . . ."

Indications are that Hubbell paid very little for this big parcel of land. The greater part of the area still belongs to the Hubbells and is one of the most valuable industrial districts in the city of Des Moines.

Real estate was only one of Hubbell's early fields of activity. He was one of four men who built the first Des Moines streetcar line in 1866. The Equitable came into being under his sponsorship in 1867. The first Des Moines waterworks was organized in 1871.

Polk and Hubbell also were experts at picking up defunct properties. They handled the liquidation of the B. F. Allen bankruptcy. The failure of Allen, leading Des Moines banker, was a major financial disaster.

The "perpetual" diary and the other papers provide brief glimpses into the widening Hubbell power and influence in the 1860's and 1870's. As explained before, however, the diary consists largely of one-line business reminders, family comments and social notes. On February 13, 1866, Hubbell wrote: "F. W. Palmer note $186.92 due." Palmer then was editor of the Iowa State Register. He evidently had borrowed some money from Hubbell.

On July 5, 1874, the diary reports that Fred's brother, Solon Hubbell, "absconded with $500 of the Equitable's money." Solon never came back. He was drowned in November of that year in the Mississippi River at St. Louis.

Tradition has it that Fred Hubbell proposed marriage to Florence Cooper soon after coming to Des Moines in 1861. Florence, a great beauty of her time, did not accept. She later married a Mr. Ginn. Florence was a daughter of Isaac Cooper and a sister of Frances Cooper. Fred married Frances March 19, 1863. The marriage took place in Isaac's home. The Register carried a story of the event. The story said in part: "Our best wishes go with the happy pair. The 19th of March, although dark and dismal to most folks, brought sunshine and happiness to our young friends. May that sunshine and happiness remain with them forever."

Hubbell did not have the cash immediately available to buy Frances a wedding ring. He did own lots on High Street. He sold the lots and bought some gold. He had the ring made to order from the gold.

How much did it cost a prosperous Des Moines couple to live in those days? Apparently well under $100 a month, except when unusual expenses were incurred. Hubbell listed what appears to be the family expenses for nine months of 1865. Here they are: January $104.92, February $69.69, March $56.50, April $83.20, May $467.06, June $98.68, July $107.35, August $102.80, September $52.88.

The expense for May may have been high because Fred and Frances started housekeeping for themselves that month. Perhaps the $467.06 in part, represents purchase of furniture and household equipment. And doctor bills as well. The Hubbells were a family of three by this time. Frederick Cooper Hubbell arrived April 29, 1864. The diary for the date says only: "Little Freddie born."

— 7 —

Narrow Gauge

THE TOWN OF Jefferson, Iowa, population 1,000, was thrilled. A new instrument for prosperity had arrived. Said the Greene County Gazette: "The snort of the narrow gauge was heard and the iron horse invaded our city streets on Monday . . . after work by night, day and Sunday, and we gladly welcome it."

The year was 1882. The narrow gauge railroad had reached Jefferson from Des Moines. At last Jefferson had a direct rail connection with the capital of Iowa. Frederick M. Hubbell was a key figure in the building that railroad, and of at least one other Iowa narrow gauge line of the 19th century.

The narrow gauge railroad of those bygone days is all but forgotten now. Yet, in their time, those "pony" railroads were a wonderful thing.

It is hard to appreciate now how vital all railroads, big and little, were to the people of Iowa 70 and 80 years ago. There were no automobiles or trucks, no highways as we know them. Streets in the largest cities were wretchedly muddy in rainy weather. The mud roads out in the country were impassable in some seasons. Everybody had to stay home when heavy rain fell or the snow melted.

The railroads spectacularly advanced civilization in pioneer America by providing steady and sure transportation in all kinds of weather.

Communications were as vital then as they are now. The pioneer had to get his hogs and cattle to market, just as the modern farmer does. And in return, the early settler also needed the goods and services of the city and town.

It wasn't easy for many sparsely settled areas to get railroads. Building a road was expensive and operating costs were high. Railroads frequently failed financially, even when such experts as Jefferson S. Polk and Fred Hubbell were involved in the management.

States, counties and cities put on vigorous campaigns to attract railroads. The federal government gave them huge tracts of land as subsidies. Settlers often voted tax money to be paid to the railroad companies upon completion of a rail line into their county. The people of Greene County, Iowa, for example, voted a "5% tax" on property in the county in 1881 for railroad purposes. The tax was supposed to produce $27,-814 for the railroad company in 1882.

A narrow gauge line had a gauge of three feet. That is, the distance from one rail across to the other was three feet. The gauge on the standard railroad

Four men were killed and many injured in a narrow gauge railroad wreck south of Jefferson, Iowa. The reward never was claimed.

$1,000 REWARD!

The Des Moines North-western Railway Company will pay a Reward of One Thousand Dollars for the arrest and conviction of the person or persons who placed the Obstruction on its track, in Franklin township, on the 26th of September, 1881, which wrecked the train that day.

Said Company will also pay a reward of $300 for the arrest and conviction of any person placing Obstructions on its track whereby the trains have or may be impeded.

J. S. POLK,
President.

JEFFERSON SCOTT POLK, early Des Moines attorney, who was Hubbell's law partner.

A train passing through Polk County in post-Civil War era.

was then, and is now, four feet and eight and one-half inches. The narrow gauge lines thus had smaller cars and smaller engines. They were much cheaper to operate and to maintain.

The narrow gauge railroad was looked upon with much favor in the so-called "feeder line" territory in Iowa in the 1870's and 1880's. Such territory, it was felt, could not support a full-sized railroad. Yet, there was enough freight and passenger business in many of these areas to justify narrow gauge service.

The narrow gauge right-of-way didn't require so much grading as was needed for the big railroads. Lighter (and less expensive) rails were used. The bridges were smaller and cheaper. The Scranton, Iowa, Journal of April 8, 1881, said the operating cost at that time for a standard gauge averaged $4,355 a mile. The newspaper said the average expense for a narrow gauge was only $338.85 a mile. It doesn't seem possible now that the expense of operating a narrow gauge would have been that much below that of the standard gauge. Yet, the difference undoubtedly was substantial. One authority says the cost of constructing a narrow gauge line was less than 40 per cent of the standard gauge.

The narrow gauge had one big comparative advantage. Back in the 1880's, railroads had a rule against loading more than 10 tons cargo on a car. The limit was the same for both big cars and little cars. The narrow gauge could carry 10 tons on each car almost as well as the standard gauge could. Thus, narrow gauge transportation was much cheaper—until the limit on standard cars was increased to 30, 40 and 50 tons, where it should have been all the time.

In the end, the narrow gauge service disappeared. Narrow gauge cars could not be used on standard lines going into the Chicago market. For example, a load of hogs coming into Jefferson on a narrow gauge line had to be reloaded on a standard gauge car for shipment into Chicago on the North Western Railroad. That trans-shipment meant added, and unnecessary, expense.

The big railroads, however, learned a valuable lesson in efficient use of freight cars from the narrow gauge group. The pony lines taught the big ones that the 10-ton freight limit was too low.

For upwards of 30 years, Hubbell was deep in railroading. He was a key man in the building, financing and operation of three railroads. These roads connected Des Moines with Ames, with Boone and with Fonda. He also had some connection with a fourth line between Des Moines and Albia.

In addition, he was a leader in the organization of the Des Moines Union Railway, a terminal and switching line in Des Moines. With the exception of Grenville Dodge of Council Bluffs, famed builder of the Union Pacific, no Iowan in history had so much experience with railroad promotion as Hubbell—or made so much money at it.

In the late 1860's, the future of the narrow gauge seemed bright. Said one authority: "In 1865 a narrow gauge craze struck Des Moines. The big roads cost too much money. The pony road could be built on top of the ground to every man's farm and into every town. A system of these roads was concocted radiating from Des Moines to the adjoining states at every point on the compass. J. S. Polk with his usual faith in the city, Fred M. Hubbell and others organized the Des Moines and Minnesota and started for St. Paul and south as far as it could go."

The Des Moines and Minnesota came to a quick and rather sad end. The company collapsed after some grading had been done both north and south of Des Moines. The portion of the road from Des Moines to Ames was sold at sheriff's sale to Polk & Hubbell.

In 1870, the Des Moines and Minneapolis Railroad was organized. Polk & Hubbell again assumed the financing. So eager were the farmers and townspeople between Des Moines and Ames for the railroad that they voted $118,000 in tax subsidies. The North Western refused to accept the subsidy money as a reward for connecting Des Moines with that railroad's main line at Ames.

Troubles then piled up fast for the Des Moines and Minneapolis. Taxpayers went into court to halt payment of the subsidies to the Des Moines and Minneapolis. In the end, the company failed. A reorganization was ordered. The new officers of the company were: Samuel Merrill (former governor of Iowa), president; Fred Hubbell, secretary; and James Callanan, treasurer.

The line's outlook was rosy again by January 12, 1874. A ceremony was arranged. A big crowd gathered on the east side in Des Moines (probably at about the present intersection of East Walnut Street and the North Western tracks) to see Gov. Cyrus C. Carpenter drive the first spike. Construction again was started.

By July 1 of 1874, the road had been completed to Ames. The cost was $300,000. Many farmers along the way had been induced to subscribe subsidies to the line. Once again, however, the railroad came to grief. Says one historian: "The line of track was largely the serpentine line of subscriptions. (The road) soon became embarrassed. Subscriptions were repudiated, thousands of lawsuits were begun and its stock went down to zero."

In 1879, the North Western bought the line and changed the gauge to standard. The first North Western passenger train on the broad track entered Des Moines July 11, 1880. (The North Western still uses the same route from Des Moines to Ames but only for freight.)

This was not Des Moines' first standard-gauge rail service, of course. The old Des Moines Valley Railroad from Keokuk was completed into Des Moines in 1866. The Rock Island reached Des Moines from Davenport in 1871.

Hubbell was not hurt by the failure of the Des Moines and Minneapolis, to any substantial extent at least. He and his partner, Polk, by that time, were up to their ears in a half dozen other projects, including railroads.

The articles of incorporation of the Narrow Gauge Railway Construction Company were filed in Des Moines January 14, 1880. Hubbell was president, J. S. Clarkson was vice-president. John S. Runnells was secretary and Jefferson Polk was treasurer. The authorized capital stock was $1,000,000. Clarkson was editor of the Iowa State Register. Runnells was a famous railroad man after whom the town of Runnells is named.

Even bigger names were coming into Hubbell's life at the same time. Such names as General Dodge of Council Bluffs, Jay Gould, one of the top railroad manipulators of all time, and Russell Sage, who was a 19th century railroad baron second only to Gould.

Builders

EVERY STUDENT OF American history knows about the ruthless and bold Jay Gould. It was said that he controlled 10,000 miles of railroads in 1880.

He is best recalled now for his unsuccessful attempt to corner the market on free gold. That attempt resulted in a nationwide panic September 24, 1869. The day still is known in history as "Black Friday." That is another story, however.

Gould's principal interests (and machinations) involved such large railroads as the Erie, the Wabash and the Union Pacific. He also had grandiose plans for narrow gauges. One such plan sounded good for Iowa.

Gould owned a barge line on the Mississippi River between St. Louis and New Orleans. He proposed making St. Louis the hub of a system of narrow gauge railroads extending into the western farm country. The narrow gauges would carry grain and other commodities from Iowa and elsewhere to St. Louis. The barges would transport the commodities down the river to ocean vessels at New Orleans. Thus, the cost of exporting farm products to Europe would be greatly reduced.

This method was supposed to save as much as 10 cents a bushel on shipments of Iowa grain to European markets. The usual route for such shipments in those days either was all the way by rail to the New York port, or by rail to Chicago and the rest of the way to the Atlantic seaboard by way of the Great Lakes and the Erie Canal.

Commenting on the prospective reduction in shipping costs, the Scranton, Iowa Journal said: "Now if the farmers received only a fifth of that saving, what would it amount to in the course of a few years on the grain market? What would be the profit to the farmers of Scranton township if they received 2 cents a bushel more for their wheat? . . . The question may be asked: 'How will the narrow gauge secure to us these advantages?' We answer, by giving us direct connection with the 'Fighting Wabash' in Des Moines."

The "Fighting Wabash" was Gould's Wabash, St. Louis and Pacific Railroad.

Wheat sold for 75 cents a bushel at Scranton in the spring of 1881. The price of both corn and oats was 20 cents a bushel. At the same time, wheat was worth about $1 in Chicago. Corn varied from 37 to 40 cents in Chicago and oats were 31 to 34 cents. Iowa farmers who had to sell at those prices were much interested in any plan which promised them a saving of even two cents a bushel in shipping costs.

The Scranton Journal also said the narrow gauge plan offered a "happy escape from the tyranny of unjust discrimination so clearly manifest in the railroad manipulations of the east." Iowans in those days often were profoundly convinced that the railroads bilked shippers on freight charges to Chicago and New York.

Some narrow gauge lines were built in a St. Louis system, with Gould in the background. St. Louis did get a lot of railroad-and-river business. The hope and expectation of building a system that would bypass Chicago and New York, however, did not work out to any substantial extent.

The records show that Gould owned securities in Iowa narrow gauge lines with which Hubbell was identified. Russell Sage also owned securities in those lines. The names of both Gould and Sage appear frequently in the Hubbell diaries.

Gould and Sage "took" a lot of people in their lifetimes. But they didn't "take" Frederick M. Hubbell. It may well be that he "took" them. Hubbell protected his own interests so well that when the Milwaukee completed purchase of two lines in 1898 he realized $1,827,500 from the transaction.

Frederick C. Hubbell was his father's closest associate and adviser in those early years (and later as well). Frederick C. once said: "I've seen my father sit down in meetings with the giants of his time. He was the equal of any of them."

Frederick C. Hubbell was a highly competent individual in his own right. His activities in railroads, insurance and banking contributed substantially to the growth of the Hubbell estate.

The Hubbell railroad story is complicated—and fascinating. For 30 years the Hubbell diary is a maze of construction details; of heavy financing in New York, Chicago and Des Moines; of debts, deals, offers and counter offers. Many of the diary entries are too complicated for present-day understanding.

Fred Hubbell was a party to the construction and operation of two Iowa narrow gauge railroads in the 1880s. One such line was the "Des Moines Northwestern" between Des Moines and Fonda, Iowa, a distance of 113.8 miles. This was the narrow gauge that reached Jefferson, Iowa, in 1882.

The Des Moines-to-Fonda line was the longest narrow gauge railroad ever built in Iowa. That line was along the present Milwaukee route from Des Moines to Spirit Lake, Iowa.

The second narrow gauge was built from Clive, which is just west of Des Moines, to Boone. That is a distance of 34.97 miles. This line was the "St. Louis, Des Moines and Northern."

Hubbell apparently did not have much to do with another railroad which connected Des Moines and

Albia, Iowa. This railroad first was known as the "Des Moines, Albia and Knoxville." Later it became the "Des Moines & St. Louis."

Hubbell also was the organizing force in the formation of the Des Moines Union Railway Company, which provided station and other terminal facilities in Des Moines. Both the Fonda and Boone lines were to have been much longer railroads. The Fonda line was to have been extended to Sioux Falls, S. D. The Boone line was to have reached the northern border of Iowa through Boone, Hamilton, Wright, Hancock and Winnebago counties. These extensions, however, never materialized.

The Fonda and Boone lines, changed to standard gauge, finally were merged under the name of the "Des Moines, Northern and Western Railway Company." The Milwaukee, which bought the lines in 1898, still serves those areas, though not with passenger trains. The Milwaukee already owned a 40 per cent interest in the lines in 1898. What the Milwaukee did was to buy the other 60 per cent in the final purchase.

That 1898 transaction was the culmination of a long period of activity by Hubbell and his associates in 19th century railroading. This period began with the "Narrow Gauge Railway Construction Company" and the "Wabash Syndicate."

The construction company was formed in 1879 in Des Moines. This company (and its corporate successor) built the Fonda and Boone lines for the "Wabash Syndicate." The Fonda line was completed in 1881 and the Boone line in 1882.

As mentioned before, the Wabash railroad was controlled by Jay Gould. The "Wabash Syndicate" was a loosely organized group which was sponsored by the Wabash Railroad. Grenville Dodge, Polk & Hubbell, Clarkson, Runnells, A. B. Cummins and other Iowans seem to have been part of the syndicate. Most of the group also were in the Narrow Gauge Railway Construction Company, of which Hubbell was president. The groups are so inter-mixed that it is difficult to tell where one began and the other left off.

The construction company was the original owner of the Fonda line. The line was leased in 1881 by the "Des Moines Northwestern" to the "Wabash, St. Louis & Pacific" for 99 years. It appears that the construction company leased the line to the "Des Moines Northwestern" which in turn leased the property to the Wabash.

Grenville Dodge of Council Bluffs was the "front man" for "Wabash Syndicate" in Iowa. Dodge was close to Gould. Dodge, in fact, was Gould's contact man in dealings with the federal government in the 1870s.

Dodge's letters in the 1880s indicate that he personally put up much of the money used in construction of the Fonda and Boone lines. If he did put up much cash, he lost part of it. The lines were not profitable until they had gone through periods of reorganization.

A December 3, 1881 letter from Hubbell to Dodge indicates that Dodge was providing the construction money for the narrow gauges. The letter says in part: "I now enclose vouchers to the amount of $6,214 which please examine as soon as possible and if found correct have the amount placed to the credit of Polk & Hubbell at the Park bank and oblige."

A December 22 letter the same year from Hubbell to Dodge warned: ". . . if the bills are not paid here, the work will stop and the contractors will begin to file liens on the property . . . it is impossible for this company to furnish money to build the road, and if you decide not to furnish it, the work will have to stop." The money must have been forthcoming. The road was completed. The letters were addressed to Dodge at his New York office.

The Boone line had been incorporated separately in 1881. Clarkson was president; Runnells vice president; Polk secretary and Hubbell treasurer. The Des Moines Union Railway Company was incorporated the next year with a capital stock of $1,000,000. Dodge was president; James F. Howe vice president and Hubbell secretary-treasurer.

Clarkson seems to have been the principal force in the construction of the line to Albia. That railroad was built by the "Des Moines and St. Louis Railroad Company" which was incorporated in 1881. This line, 68.21 miles, was built in 1881 and 1882 and was leased to the Wabash. Hubbell may have been involved in this project. He is not listed as an officer of the company, however.

It is entirely possible that the slates of officers of all these companies were, for the most part, "fronts" for Dodge, Gould and others. Polk & Hubbell appear to have had complete supervision over actual building of at least the Fonda and Boone lines.

The expense of building the railroads seems to have been met through bonds issued by the operating company. For example, the Boone line was authorized to deliver up to $8,000 a mile in bonds to the construction company.

The outcome of all this was: The Fonda and Boone lines were built; at least one of the companies went through a mortgage foreclosure and both companies were reorganized; in the reorganization, the "Wabash Syndicate" seems to have faded out of the picture; the name "St. Louis" was dropped; the Fonda and Boone lines were merged into one company.

Polk & Hubbell and, later, Hubbell alone emerged as a major bondholder of the reorganized railroad properties in the 1890s. Dodge also held quite a block of the securities. Hubbell and Dodge really ran the railroad. Gould and Sage had relatively small holdings.

Sage apparently held a substantial interest in the Des Moines-to-Albia line. Hubbell conferred frequently with both Gould and Sage on trips to New York in the 1880s and early 1890s.

It was the name of Gould that quickened the Iowa pulse when the Boone line was in the planning stage. Describing the proposed line from Clive to Boone, the Boone Standard of April 9, 1881 said: "Back of and holding the steering oar in this system is that wonderful organizer, Jay Gould, whose hand placed to any project immediately causes a shower of gold . . . This is our golden opportunity to get out of the woods and make Boone what it ought to be."

Incidentally, railroading was a slow-motion proposition on the narrow gauge lines in those days. One 1882 schedule called for a passenger train to leave Jefferson at 6 p.m. and to arrive in Adel at 9:32. That's more than 3½ hours for a rail distance that did not exceed 45 miles.

Jay Gould wasn't so popular in Iowa (or anywhere else) after the narrow gauge lines were completed. The Wabash was in receivership. The receiver operated the Fonda and Albia lines. Gould, Sage and the other rail barons were under heavy attack.

Through the columns of the Iowa State Register, Clarkson sought in 1883 to build up Iowa sentiment for Gould. Clarkson carried a story January 17, 1883 saying that Gould was planning a huge coal-mining enterprise in Iowa. The story said in part: "It may be safely assumed that the headquarters of this great mining scheme will be in Des Moines, thus adding another enterprise of abundant capital to this city . . . Meantime, it will be enough for our people to know that there are the best grounds for believing that Jay Gould is about to put a large plant of business capital in this region, with this city made headquarters for it. He is a good man to be interested in Des Moines and to aid in prodding its development, increasing its wealth and advancing its power."

The big mining project never materialized, under Gould's sponsorship at least. Clarkson undoubtedly thought it was coming, however. Clarkson was strong for such men as Dodge and Gould. The editor firmly believed they made a substantial contribution to the development of Iowa by promoting railroads for the undeveloped areas of this state.

Clarkson also was strong for his friend and associate, Fred Hubbell, who, with his partner Polk, was so prominent in the actual construction of narrow gauge lines into Des Moines.

—9—

Student of Railroads

HUBBELL OBVIOUSLY WAS only one of a number of persons interested in the Fonda and Boone lines before those railroads were built. Most of the capital for those lines appears to have come from Dodge, Gould and the Wabash Railroad.

Indeed, Hubbell himself in 1888 said the Fonda line was "formerly a part of the Wabash, St. Louis and Pacific system."

How did Hubbell manage in the end to gain a controlling interest over these Iowa railroads? Here is a probable explanation: First, he studied the railroad situation closely. He knew within a few dollars what every line was worth. Iowa never has had a more painstaking student of the railroad business than Frederick M. Hubbell.

Then, he kept his eyes open for bargains in railroad securities. Between 1883 and the mid-1890s, various holders of railroad securities found themselves in need of money. Hubbell either would buy from them, or would lend money on bonds posted as security. Some of those bonds inevitably became his.

HOYT SHERMAN

WESLEY REDHEAD

B. F. ALLEN

GEN. GRENVILLE DODGE

DEMOINE HOUSE, an early hotel, was on the southwest corner of First and Walnut streets, where the main Des Moines post office now is located.

As a result, an August 17, 1891 report showed the following ownership of stock in the Des Moines and Northwestern Railway Company: F. M. Hubbell, 3,250 shares; F. M. Hubbell, Son & Company, 3,249 shares; G. M. Dodge, 3,500 shares; L. M. Martin, F. C. Hubbell, A. N. Denman, H. D. Thompson and A. B. Cummins, one share apiece. Thus, the majority of the stock obviously was in the hands of the Hubbells. Fred Hubbell was president and Thompson, his close friend and associate, was treasurer.

From the beginning, Fred was no casual bystander in the building and the operation of the railroads. He kept close track of what was going on. On January 9, 1881, he wrote this information in his diary: "Des Moines & Northwestern has the following cars: Box cars 25, flat cars 18, stock cars 12, hand cars 6, passenger cars 2, caboose cars 2." Note that the railroad at that time had only two passenger cars.

Hubbell also reported that the Ohio Falls, Ohio, Car Works was building for the Des Moines & Northwestern: "Box cars 25 @ $325 each, stock cars 10 @ $325 each, flat cars 10 @ $240 each."

He even kept count of the railroad ties used on the Fonda line. On August 1, 1881, he said, "the company bought 15,000 ties.that will be loaded and shipped this week. The mill will saw 3,000 this week."

He reported each day's progress in track-building to Fonda. On November 25, 1881, he said, "the track reached 'Young's Farm'." On November 29, the track had reached "Widow Margaret Hindel." On December 12, he wrote: "One half mile today. End of track within ¼ mile of Calhoun County line. No track this a.m. because engine failed . . ."

He even listed these payments to farmers whose land was taken for railroad purposes: "Phil Roberts $50, Ben Mitchell $40, Frank Plaine $25, William Jackson $30, Isham Reynolds $25 and O. Heardley $25."

On April 1, 1881, Hubbell reported that "L. W. Reynolds and Brainard of Boone" had come to Des Moines. The diary reported that "they want a railroad bad." The next day Hubbell and the others "signed articles of incorporation for the St. Louis, Des Moines & Northern railroad," which later was the Boone line.

On June 27, 1882, Hubbell jubilantly reported that the railroad had reached Boone. He wrote in his diary that track "was laid across the Chicago and North Western and into our depot grounds tonight."

Meanwhile, the railroads were having quite a struggle. The narrow gauge lines scratched everywhere for business. When the Boone line was having its troubles in 1883, Superintendent C. F. Meek wrote to Dodge: "Weather is getting more settled, and we will have excursions to High Bridge as often as profitable. I think we can make quite a business of this."

Des Moines people evidently had a wonderful time going on railroad excursions to High Bridge near Madrid in those days. Late in the summer of 1883, Meek reported to Dodge: "I arranged a celebration at High Bridge for July 4. We handled 3,500 people from Des Moines and Boone to the Bridge on that day, giving us revenue of $1,750. We shall have excursions to the Bridge every evening during the moonlight periods this summer and every Sunday."

The railroad evidently collected 50 cents per person for the High Bridge excursions. That was equivalent to $1 or $1.50 today. The excursion revenue wasn't enough, however, to prevent foreclosure.

The Boone line wasn't alone in its financial troubles. A number of individuals were in difficulties too. (Not Hubbell, of course!) Runnells was one person with problems. He met Hubbell in New York August 21, 1883. The diary says Hubbell and Runnells "went to Trinity Churchyard to talk."

Runnells confessed in the churchyard that his personal affairs were such he had to have some money. "Told him I could do nothing until I went home," the Hubbell diary says. "When I return home I would see what I could do."

The diary doesn't say whether Hubbell helped Runnells. But an entry for August 3, 1883, or 18 days prior, says that Runnells and Clarkson had joint debts of $62,000 and Runnells individually was $31,500 in debt. Polk & Hubbell were major creditors. Clarkson and Runnells owed Polk & Hubbell $13,000 and Runnells himself owed the law firm $12,000.

Clarkson apparently was close to the edge also. Runnells again called on Hubbell November 4. Fred wrote in his diary: "He (Runnells) says that Ret Clarkson endorsed most all his papers and that he will have to give up his homestead to save Ret and Co." ("Ret" was Clarkson's nickname.)

It is not known whether Hubbell bailed out Runnells and Clarkson. He may have. They vanquished their troubles in some way. Both were prominent and successful for many years after 1883. Runnells later moved to Chicago and became president of the Pullman Company.

Incidentally, Hubbell did not limit his efforts to buying and accumulating railroad securities. He sold when he thought such securities were overvalued, or when he didn't like the looks of things in a company. He spent three whole days in New York in August of 1883 selling Wabash bonds. He sold $5,000 worth at 67 and another $5,000 at 68. He authorized a broker to sell $10,000 at 69 and an additional $10,000 at 70. The diary does not report whether the last two sales ever were made.

Even though the Boone line was in deep trouble (which led to foreclosure proceedings beginning in 1884), the owners of the line were constantly besieged to extend its track. A campaign was waged in the middle 1880s to extend the line from Boone to Clear Lake, a distance of 86 miles. Localities along the proposed right-of-way voted subsidies totaling $88,423.

Marion township in Hamilton County voted $5,-228. Webster City agreed to donate two public squares and cash of $35,000. Other subsidies voted were: Wall Lake Township, $5,835; Blaine Township, $7,394; Grimes Township, $3,176; Union Township, $5,587; Clear Lake Township, $6,496; Clear Lake Village, $7,231. Wall Lake and Blaine Townships are in Wright County, the others in Cerro Gordo County.

These subsidies never had to be paid. They lapsed when the road was not started by December 1, 1887.

The record indicates that the Fonda line went through the foreclosure wringer just as the Boone line did.

The fact that the two lines were narrow gauge seems to have been a major cause of their financial troubles. As early as 1883, the promoters and operators were getting estimates as to what it would cost to change the Boone line to standard gauge. On May 28, 1886, Superintendent Meek wrote to Dodge as follows about the Fonda line: "You know what the resources of that road are, or would be were it a standard gauge. The coal business alone could be increased four times, to say nothing of the increased advantage in livestock, hay, etc., which it is extremely difficult to handle to the satisfaction of shippers when going through."

The track was broadened to standard gauge on the Fonda line in 1891 and perhaps before that on the Boone line.

The Hubbell diaries show that Fred constantly negotiated with his various associates on railroad financing. On June 5, 1890, he tried to make a deal with Dodge in New York. "I offered Dodge $500,000 in 4% bonds for the Boone line," Hubbell wrote. "They wanted $750,000 . . . I start home tonight."

The Wabash held a sizable mortgage debt on the Fonda line in 1889. Hubbell tried to make a deal on that debt. He asked for "an extension of time on the . . . debt or leave to buy rails and ties and make the cost thereof a first lien on the road." This was for the purpose of broadening the track to standard gauge.

Wabash officials at first said they would take a new mortgage at $12,000 per mile and 5 per cent interest. They changed their minds in the negotiations, however. "My trip (to New York) was a failure," Hubbell wrote in his diary.

How the Fonda line's mortgage problem was met, the diary doesn't say. But it was met in some way. Hubbell was most astute. He may have been the most persuasive bigtime businessman Iowa ever has seen.

Every once in a while he impressed New Yorkers with a business deal. On February 5, 1890, he ar-

ranged an option with a man named Ashley on some
railroad bonds.

"Showed it (the option) to Dodge," the diary says.
"He was delighted and wanted me to close it that night.
I went back to 195 Broadway but Ashley had gone to
the train. I found him in Grand Central depot where
I paid him $10,000. Accepted his offer and got a re-
ceipt."

In 1890, Hubbell tried in New York to arrange a
deal by which Dodge would buy the Albia-to-Des
Moines line from Gould. This was the "Des Moines
& St. Louis Ry." Dodge and Gould were associates
most of the time but evidently were adversaries in business on occasions.

Dodge told Hubbell "not to offer more than $325,-
000" for the Albia line. Hubbell then went to see
Gould, who was cold to the proposition. "He (Gould)
thought $400,000 was cheap enough," the diary says.
Russell Sage also was in on the ownership of the Albia
line. On September 10, 1890, Hubbell called on Sage.

"Told him I wanted to buy ½ of Des Moines and
St. L. to Harvey, Iowa," Hubbell wrote. Harvey is in
Marion County southeast of Des Moines. Hubbell and
Sage dickered for several months after that. Although
the diary doesn't say so, the deal appears to have fallen
through.

Hubbell suffered frequent setbacks of that caliber.
But he patiently and constantly improved his position

each year in all the companies with which he was associated. And he usually ended up in control.

In 1894, the Des Moines Northern and Western Railway Company went through a mortgage foreclosure. This railroad owned the Boone and Fonda lines and trackage rights over the Des Moines Union in Des Moines. Dodge, Frederick M. Hubbell and Frederick C. Hubbell bought the line at foreclosure sale.

A memorandum in the diary shows that Hubbell was by far the controlling force in the line at the time of foreclosure. The Hubbell interests owned $2,770,-000 bonds on the Fonda line and Dodge owned $743,-000. Nobody else owned any.

Another tabulation, presumably for the Boone line, listed the Hubbells as owning $2,005,000 bonds. All other owners possessed $765,000. Russell Sage was listed for $145,000.

The new firm established by the Hubbells in the middle 1890s for the railroad properties was the "Des Moines Northern and Western Railroad Company." This company appears to have had $2,915,000 in outstanding bonds. The Hubbell interests owned $2,121,-000. Dodge owned only $271,000 and Sage $46,000. Hubbell was in complete command.

Hubbell apparently sold some of the bonds to the Milwaukee Railroad within the next year. Dodge wrote on June 10, 1895, that "the Milwaukee road owns 40 per cent of the company and has the option of taking a controlling interest, which I suppose in the proper time they will do." The Milwaukee could not have acquired 40 per cent of the railroad without buying some of Hubbell's securities.

The Hubbell diaries frequently touch on one early railroad practice that no longer is allowed. It is illegal now for a railroad to give a free pass to anybody. That was not true 50 or more years ago. Railroads gave passes lavishly, and often thereby controlled legislators, government officials and delegates to political conventions.

Hubbell was in Chicago February 17, 1897. He went to see an unnamed railroad official. "He promised me 100 passes and annuals (annual passes) for the Booge boys," the diary says. Hubbell does not record which railroad it was. James E. and H. D. Booge lived in Sioux City. James E., who founded the packing-house industry in Sioux City, was Hubbell's brother-in-law. Booge married Annie Hubbell, Fred's sister. She died in 1864 but Hubbell always remained on friendly terms with the Booges, even to the point of getting free railroad passes for them.

Hubbell later also tried to obtain passes for the Booges on the Milwaukee but Roswell Miller, the president, said no.

The diaries show that Hubbell spent fantastically small amounts of money on his many trips east. That was not only because he was thrifty. It didn't cost him anything to ride on a train. He was a railroad magnate in his own right and he had passes to go everywhere.

On March 10, 1897, he went to Chicago on an overnight trip. The diary says he had total expenses of $2.50 on that trip. It may be that he didn't have to pay for his Pullman berth. Even in 1897, however, going to Chicago and back for $2.50 was an unheard-of feat.

Another practice of the 1890s that no longer is permitted was rate-cutting on freight. There was bitter competition among the railroads in those days for each other's "through business." On April 3, 1894, Hubbell contacted a Mr. Hooper of the Great Western Railroad and told him "he could have our Chicago grain business by allowing us 40%. He asked how long a contract we would make. I told him one year at 40% and if they would allow us 45% I would make it for 10 years."

A week later, Fred met a Mr. Woodworth of the Iowa Central (now M. & St. L.) in Chicago. The diary relates: "He said all grain hauled by us to Madrid passing through the elevator there and then shipped via the Iowa Central, he would allow us 42½% and wanted me to have a circular issued to that effect to all shippers." Hubbell did not record whether he finally arranged the deals with the Great Western and the Iowa Central. All railroads did such things, however. Federal and state regulations prohibit such practices now.

As the decade of the 1890s drew near to a close, Hubbell wanted to get out of the railroad business. He was in negotiations with the Milwaukee, which had an option on his Fonda and Boone line holdings. At one point, he wrote: "If they are not going to exercise their option, we want to know it. We prefer to close out now so that Fred can go into the insurance business." (Fred was his son, Frederick C. Hubbell.)

On November 2, 1898, Hubbell wrote himself this reminder of the things he wanted if the railroad sale went through: "We want to protect employees (of the railroad). We want annuals for life on the entire system."

Whether he got the annual passes for life or not, he sold to the Milwaukee. An entry in the diary December 29, 1898, says: "Arrived in New York. Sold the 2150 bonds to the Chicago M. and St. P. Ry. Co. and it all adds up to $1,827,500. Deposited at Park bank. Loaned Metropolitan 2% on call $250,000." Hubbell received 85 cents on the dollar for the bonds.

The sale of those bonds did not mark the end of Hubbell's railroad career. There was still the Des Moines Union. Also, in the early 1890s he invested heavily in the Texas Southern Railroad, in the Gulf & Interstate, which also was located in Texas, and in another line then known as the Kansas City, Mexican and Orient Railroad.

Hubbell and his son Fred spent considerable time in Beaumont and Houston, Texas, and in Kansas City and St. Louis on transactions involving these railroads. The Hubbells apparently did not lose any money and they probably made some, although the Texas Southern did go through receivership. The diary says that at one time the Hubbells owned $409,000 in Texas Southern bonds, or 55 per cent of the total outstanding.

Regarding the Des Moines Union Railway Company, the Hubbells were defendants in the first part of the 20th century in one of the longest railroad lawsuits on record. At stake was control of the Des Moines Union.

That company provides switching trackage and facilities for railroads serving Des Moines industries and other shippers. The Hubbell-owned Des Moines Terminal Company provides similar facilities to industries in "Factory Addition," which is south of the downtown Des Moines business district.

The Des Moines Union was incorporated in 1884. Frederick M. Hubbell was one of the original incorporators. In 1890 he acquired control. He and his associates held 62½ per cent of the company's securities.

The Milwaukee and Wabash railroads filed suit against the Hubbells in 1907. Frederick C. Hubbell was president of the Des Moines Union. The plaintiffs insisted that under an old 1882 agreement the

Hubbells could only hold the Des Moines Union property in trust for the Milwaukee and the Wabash.

The case was not finally disposed of until 1920, or 13 years later. The United States Supreme Court in that year upheld the position of the Milwaukee and the Wabash. The decision in effect was that the Hubbells only held the property in trust for the two railroads.

At stake in the long battle was more than seven million dollars, five million of which was in railroad property. The final settlement awarded the Hubbells $320,000 for salaries and services. This was a major setback for F. M. Hubbell. But you never would know it from reading his diary. He laconically wrote December 6, 1920: "Parrish (his attorney) received telegram today that our Des Moines Union suit in Washington, D. C., has been decided against us. . . . Banquet of Greater Des Moines committee at Des Moines Club. Wilchinski and Sherman were the hosts. I attended."

Another (and later) court decision said that the facilities of the Des Moines Terminal Company must be leased forever to the Des Moines Union. The Union pays $1.20 for each loaded car brought upon or taken from the Des Moines Terminal tracks. Under terms of the lease, the minimum annual rental is $12,000 a year. The maximum is $18,000. The rent has been running about $15,000 annually in recent years.

Another Hubbell property is the Des Moines Western Railway Company. That company owns switching and track facilities on the east side in Des Moines. These facilities are under lease to the Fort Dodge, Des Moines & Southern Railway. The latter railroad also leases main line sidings from the Des Moines Western.

Why did Fred Hubbell sell the Fonda and Boone lines? For two reasons, probably. One was that he may have decided the future was not bright for the smaller independent railroad. The nation's big railroad systems were well established by that time. The advantages of large scale rail operations were apparent. Secondly, Hubbell never liked having his interests spread all over the country. When he sold the Fonda and Boone lines, he almost completely "returned to Des Moines" so far as his business interests were concerned.

At the beginning of the 20th century, the Hubbells controlled the Equitable. They had controlled the Des Moines Union (until the courts ruled otherwise.) Also, Hubbell's Des Moines real estate holdings and his volume of Des Moines Water Company securities both were substantial. Note that all these properties were located within the Des Moines city limits.

Except for such occasional flyers as Texas railroads, Fred Hubbell was "home to stay" businesswise for the rest of his life.

10

Polk & Hubbell

A RUMOR SPREAD rapidly over central Iowa in 1882. Along Des Moines' unpaved and muddy streets and in the town squares of such places as Jefferson, business-men stopped to discuss this startling report: "Polk & Hubbell have failed."

The rumor was not true, of course. But the report was so general that the Des Moines State Journal finally had to comment December 23, 1882. The paper called the rumor "worse than malicious."

"It could do the gentlemen (Polk & Hubbell) no harm but tends to suspicion in other quarters men unable to stand the pressure," the Journal said. "Well informed sources have told us that Polk & Hubbell have cleared over $300,000 during the past year . . ."

The newspaper story is significant in Hubbell's history because of that $300,000 figure. It is not known whether Polk & Hubbell enjoyed an income of that size in 1882. But Hubbell thought enough of the story to paste the clipping in one of his scrapbooks.

A study of the operations of Polk & Hubbell indi-cates the law firm might well have had an income reaching into six figures in 1882. They may have been the most spectacular law team Des Moines has seen in 100 years.

Polk & Hubbell were not only good lawyers, they were principally large scale financiers and promoters of major business ventures, including railroads. Des Moines hasn't had such a combination since they broke up (in somewhat of a row) in 1887.

Jefferson Scott Polk was a tall, bearded, impressive-looking man. He came to Des Moines in 1855, the same year as Hubbell. Polk then was 25, nine years older than Hubbell, and already a lawyer. (Polk was admitted to the bar in Kentucky, his home state.)

Polk was the "front man" of the law firm. Hubbell, in the background, was a solid force. In 1864, when Hubbell was still only 25, he was described as "useful and successful in getting and managing business." All his productive life, he was "useful and successful in getting and managing business."

Perhaps because Polk did, Hubbell also wore whiskers in this period. He had a set of "muttonchops." (See frontispiece.) He shaved off the whiskers sometime after 1894.

In 1866, Polk & Hubbell appear among the partners in the organization of Des Moines' first streetcar company. Dr. Mahlon P. Turner obtained the streetcar franchise. The fourth partner in the venture was U. B. White.

Mrs. Frederick M. Hubbell

This family group picture was taken about 1896. FREDERICK M. HUBBELL is seated left. ISAAC COOPER is holding JAMES W. HUBBELL on his lap. Standing right is FREDERICK W. HUBBELL. Standing rear are GROVER C. HUBBELL (left) and FREDERICK C. HUBBELL.

Des Moines had a population of perhaps 7,000 then. The first streetcar ran from the courthouse at Fifth Street east on Court Avenue to the foot of the State Capitol Hill. Usually the car was pulled by mules, although the company had some horses also.

The track was laid on mud. The franchise provided that the top speed of the streetcar should not exceed six miles an hour. The franchise never was violated. The pace, in fact, was so slow that men usually beat the streetcar by walking.

Sometimes the car would slip off the rails. Then it was up to the passengers to get off and lift it back into place. Occasionally, the mules would slip in the mud. Often they stayed on the ground resting for several minutes. Nobody tried to get them up until they were ready to rise of their own accord. It would have done no good. The line was not much of a financial success and Polk & Hubbell got out of the company in 1868.

On January 25, 1867, the Equitable Life Insurance Company of Iowa began operations. Hubbell was the first secretary. Polk was in on the organization of that company also. The Equitable story is told elsewhere in this volume.

In 1871, Polk & Hubbell organized a company to provide city water service for Des Moines. (B. F. Allen agreed to serve as President.) The waterworks was capitalized at $300,000. The company was reorganized as a stock company in 1881. The Hubbell interests were substantial holders of water company securities from 1871 until the city bought the system in 1919.

From the beginning, the waterworks has used the so-called "Holly system" of obtaining water. An early newspaper account described the system as follows: "The water is taken from large chambers excavated deep and broad under the bed of the 'Coon River. And being thus filtered gives the city the purest, the best water of any city in the Union."

The firm of Polk & Hubbell thus was involved in railroads, insurance, a streetcar company and a water company. That would have been more than enough for any ordinary partnership. But not the aggressive Polk & Hubbell. They began to acquire large holdings of real estate. Some property they bought as a firm. Other parcels were purchased individually. They were so financially strong that they were able to take over most of the B. F. Allen assets when that notable Des Moines banker went broke.

Benjamin Franklin Allen was the top ranking banker in Des Moines in the 1860's. He had been an early Des Moines merchant. He bought up a lot of property along the prospective railroad routes. He platted small cities and towns along railroads throughout central Iowa. He sold these properties and, as one historian put it, made "a pile of money."

Allen spent $250,000 in building Terrace Hill, the ancient Des Moines home on West Grand Avenue that now belongs to the Hubbells.

In the early 1870s, Allen went after bigger financial game. He bought the Cook County National Bank in Chicago. That was the mistake of his life. One historian called the bank "a sepulchre of rottenness." Allen poured all his Des Moines resources into the Chicago institution. It was no use. The bank wasn't any good. Besides, the times were against Allen. (A large-scale depression developed in 1873.) In 1875, he was adjudged bankrupt. Hoyt Sherman was appointed receiver. Polk & Hubbell were named attorneys for the liquidation.

The Allen failure was monumental. Thousands of people lost their savings in the collapse of the Allen empire.

The liquidation of the Allen assets was still very much a live issue in 1881 when the Hubbell diaries resume after the 22-year lapse.

An 1883 tabulation in the diaries shows that at the time the claims against Allen totaled $4,063,572. (That is comparable to 12 to 15 million dollars now.)

As the bankruptcy proceedings, started in 1875, slowly rolled toward a final conclusion, Polk & Hubbell had the resources to buy up at least $3,361,404 of those claims. It is not clear how much they paid for this paper. The diary, however, records court approval of a Polk & Hubbell bid of $350,000 for Allen's assets.

The records indicate that the Allen paper was worth 10 to 15 cents on the dollar in liquidation. Some of it was worth much less. On October 22, 1883, for example, Hubbell bought an E. F. Pulsifer and Co. $6,843 claim on Allen for $684. On the same day Hubbell bought another $814 certificate for $40.

Some of the paper wasn't worth even that much. Hubbell once bid $1,500 on $207,000 in Allen's indebtedness. The owner of the paper wanted $5,000. Hubbell wrote in his diary that he "wanted time to think it over." The diary does not record whether he bought that paper.

In the end, Polk & Hubbell got the bulk of the Allen assets, perhaps all that was left in the 1880s for $350,000. How they came out on that venture is not set down in the diary. They had the money to hold on to the property, however. And times improved. There is every reason to believe that they earned a good profit on the Allen assets.

The Polk & Hubbell purchases of his assets appeared to have been all right with Allen. He was stripped clean anyway. He remained friendly with Hubbell. Allen went to California where he operated a small fruit farm until his death in 1914.

The prosperity of the firm of Polk & Hubbell was accompanied by some friction between the partners. Both were alert and hard-headed. Each may have wanted to go his own way and not have to split his profits with the other. Polk was more anxious to dissolve the partnership than was Hubbell, at first at least. On February 24, 1883, Hubbell wrote: "Polk came to the office tonight to talk over the future of our firm. He wanted to know if I wanted to dissolve, etc. I told him no."

On February 25, the next day, Polk offered to take $400,000 for his interest in the firm and give Hubbell time to pay it. Hubbell would not deal.

An entry dated November 25, 1885, in the large "perpetual" diary reports that Hubbell had endorsed a note for $10,000 for Polk with the old Iowa Loan and Trust Co. in Des Moines. That transaction might have caused trouble between the partners. Many a friendship has gone on the rocks over friction resulting from endorsement of notes.

The partnership finally was dissolved December 31, 1887. The complete terms of dissolution are not now known. The Hubbell diaries for 1885, 1886 and 1887 are missing. On the day that Polk & Hubbell broke up, Hubbell formed another partnership that still exists today under the name of F. M. Hubbell, Son & Company, Incorporated. The original partners in that firm, which dealt mostly in real estate and railroad properties, were: Hubbell himself; his son, Fred C. Hubbell (then 23 years old), and H. DeVere Thompson, his longtime business associate. Mrs. Thompson and Mrs. Hubbell were sisters, both daughters of Isaac Cooper.

Polk and Hubbell took two years after 1887 to unravel their interests.

One of the few downright angry comments to appear in the Hubbell diary is to be seen under date of January 10, 1888. Hubbell headed the diary page: "Memo of Polk's unjust and unfair treatment to me." Fred then listed seven grievances. One paragraph says: "(Polk) made me sell Equitable stock at 50 cents to him or go out of partnership. After the sale, the stock was marked paid-up stock of 100 cents on the dollar for what I sold at 50c."

Other grievances were: "Made me sign articles of partnership in 1878 or 79 to give him about $3,500 a year for being his partner. Under this contract I paid the firm say $12,000 . . ." (It would appear the total amount should have been more than $12,000.) "In the William M. Jones note, he put the note on to the Equitable at par and then would not stand up to his endorsement . . . "I bought . . . 230 feet to fit out my homestead at the rate of $5,000. Polk got title in his name and made me pay him profit on the ground . . . I had to give street all around my lot and pay for grading it while the syndicate paid for all the dirt he has hauled onto his lot and he paid nothing . . ."

Meanwhile, Polk and Hubbell still owned considerable railroad and other property in common even though the partnership had come to an end. On January 29, 1888, Hubbell wrote: "If I trade with Polk on railroad, I must have:" Hubbell then listed 21 different items, including: "Narrow Gauge Railway Construction stock and books, Boone line stock and books, Des Moines Northwestern railway stock and books . . . Polk must assign attorney fees for all debts, all lots in Herndon. He must resign as treasurer (of the railroad company or companies) . . . He also must have got Hoyt Sherman stock."

Sherman still owned some Equitable stock that Hubbell wanted (and ultimately got).

The diary for July 3, 1888, says that "Polk wanted me to talk about water company and railroad. Said he wanted to sell both to me." Hubbell offered $75,000 for Polk's stock in both. Hubbell already held substantial amounts of the bonds of both companies.

On July 14, Polk said "he would take $100,000 for railroad and water stocks and take the Red Rock Coal Co. stock at $10,000." Hubbell countered with another offer which Polk "promptly rejected . . ." On December 6, Hubbell made another offer. The diary quotes Polk as saying "he did not think I wanted to buy very bad."

By December 15, tempers were getting short as a result of the negotiations. Polk threatened Hubbell with legal action if one of Fred's water companies tried to do business outside the city.

"I told him (Polk) we intended only to supply the suburbs of Des Moines with water and if he interfered with that we should lock horns," the diary says. "He reminded me of the fable of the wolf and the lamb and wanted me to consider him the lamb."

As part of the final settlement, Hubbell offered to allow Polk to be railroad president the next year. Polk was unimpressed. He said he would "cross that bridge when he came to it." Hubbell finally frankly told Polk his demands were "too high and I would not pay it, that the railroad was not worth a damn above its debts."

Agreement finally was reached on December 18, 1888. Hubbell paid $72,000 of which $10,000 was in cash, $30,000 in Hubbell's personal notes and $23,000 in other paper, such as coal stock. Polk also got a stone quarry.

Hubbell was satisfied with the settlement. He wrote: "I get his (Polk's) water stock $105,000, his railroad stock subject to Dodge's interest $500,000, the Westfall judgment $9,000, lots at Herndon, right of way, etc." One provision of the settlement was that Polk was to have "water free and (railroad) passes as long as we can give them conveniently . . ."

Thus, Polk and Hubbell finally completely parted company as business associates early in 1889.

Polk went on to achieve success in the construction of interurban lines in central Iowa. He held valuable Des Moines real estate. It was as president of the Des Moines Streetcar Company, however, that he was best known. In 1889, Des Moines had a number of independent streetcar firms, perhaps as many as seven. Each company charged a nickel for a ride. There were no transfers among the competing companies. Thus, a passenger might have to pay 15 cents to go from Highland Park to Greenwood Park.

Polk bought up all the lines and consolidated them. One fare of a nickel was all a passenger needed to cross town.

Polk also established a system whereby each streetcar carried a mailbox on the rear. If a resident came running with a letter to mail, the motorman had to stop the car. A postal clerk periodically gathered the mail from the streetcar boxes downtown.

Des Moines oldtimers remember how Polk, head bare and whiskers flying in the wind, frequently served as motorman on one of his cars in his final years.

Polk and Hubbell were on good personal terms again a few years after dissolution of their partnership. In fact, Mr. and Mrs. Polk attended the wedding of Hubbell's daughter Beulah in 1899 and brought a present.

On November 3, 1907, Hubbell wrote in his diary: "Jefferson Scott Polk died today, 76 years, 8 months, 13 days."

11

Thrift

"Now that I am maturing, I have more fun. I am not such a tightwad as I used to be. Occasionally I buy something I don't need, but I can afford it now. I don't advise anyone to do likewise until he has provided for his family and his future."

Fred Hubbell certainly was maturing when he said that. He was 86 years old!

Was he really a tightwad? His history on that topic is highly interesting.

Hubbell unquestionably was thrifty. Once again, that inner urge dates back to the 1850's in Connecticut where as a boy he was deeply impressed by the fact that the poorhouse was the ultimate destination of many good people. That recollection colored his thinking to some extent even at 86 years of age. Note in the above quotation that he advised everyone to be careful with his money "until he has provided for his family and his future."

No man in Iowa history ever provided so well as Hubbell did for "his family and his future."

In his business dealings, Hubbell got every cent that was coming to him. Business transactions were a kind of a game to him. He delighted in matching wits with other business men who presumably were able to take care of themselves.

At the same time, his gifts to charity and to civic enterprises were substantial. Opening Hubbell Avenue through northeast Des Moines, for example, cost him an estimated $95,000. Also, the Des Moines Chamber of Commerce put on a drive before 1900 for the federal government to locate an army post in Des Moines. Hubbell was chairman of the chamber's finance committee.

The committee raised $40,000 to buy the land where Fort Des Moines is now located. The land was donated to the federal government. The bill establishing the post passed congress in 1900. There are indications that Hubbell personally contributed $10,000 to the land-buying fund.

Hubbell was more than generous down through the years to the Des Moines Home for the Aged at 2833 University Avenue. He was elected president of the home for 28 consecutive years, from 1898 to 1926. (James W. Hubbell, his grandson, is president of the home now.)

In World War I, he was a big buyer of Federal Government Liberty Bonds. Such bonds were not looked upon as a lucrative investment in those days.

Money invested in other securities brought a higher return. Hubbell subscribed $100,000 to the Victory loan drive right after World War I ended. On December 19, 1918, he wrote: "Borrowed $20,000 at the Central National Bank to pay installment due today on my subscription to $100,000 of Liberty Bonds. 4¼ per cent. Fourth Loan."

Meanwhile, he was giving uncounted thousands to Drake University, Methodist Hospital, YMCA and YWCA, Roadside settlement and other civic projects. In addition, he was always giving $2 here, $20 there, $50 to help this family, $20 to help that cause. Few people knew of those gifts.

That is not the way a miser acts.

It could be that he deliberately cultivated the reputation of being a tightwad. A man of great wealth is always a target of people with causes that require money. Sometimes the causes are worthy. Often they are not. By becoming known as a hard man with a dollar, Hubbell undoubtedly saved himself a lot of badgering from solicitors seeking money. Contributing to unworthy ventures is a way of wasting money. And waste of any sort, but particularly of money, went against Hubbell's grain.

"Never spend a cent foolishly," he once said. "Economy is absolutely essential to those who want to be rich. Before anyone buys even a paper of pins, he should say, 'Can I possibly do without that?' If he can, he should save the money and put it in the bank. Dollars added to dollars make a nest egg. Interest will accumulate. Some of the money will be used to buy mortgages and property. Eventually, the savings will be earning more money for their owner than he earns for himself at his regular job."

Hubbell kept track of almost everything he spent. Back in May of 1881, for example, he took a trip to Jefferson, Iowa, on railroad business. The diary says he spent "50 cents dinner, 10 shave, Gazette 2.00 (presumably a newspaper subscription), bill at Head House (hotel) 2.25, dinner at Ackley 00." Somebody must have taken him to dinner at Ackley. The meal didn't cost him anything at least.

Oldtime Iowa Republicans will enjoy the diary's reports on Hubbell's dealings with A. B. Cummins, one of the state's alltime greats in politics. Cummins was governor of Iowa three times and United States senator three times. He also was an excellent attorney. In the 1880's and 1890's, and later as well, Cummins was Hubbell's attorney.

Hubbell was always on guard lest Cummins charge too much for his services. In 1888, for example, Hubbell was involved in a lawsuit with a company identified only as "Monarch." On September 29, the diary says: "Had a talk with Cummins today. The Monarch was mentioned incidentally but Cummins ought not charge for it."

On November 1, of that same year, Hubbell wrote: "Cummins came to my office and wanted $650 on his account. He ought not to charge for coming after his money."

One day in 1894, Cummins visited Hubbell at home. The diary says: "(Cummins) came to my house to tell me that Judge Holmes would decide the water co. case Monday morning. I asked for no advice and he ought not to charge me anything."

Hubbell never did like the idea of spending very much money for lawyers (probably partly because he was one himself). On December 2, 1892, he decided to retain Judge C. C. Cole, one of Des Moines' great legal minds of his time. The diary described this exchange between Hubbell and Cole: "Called on Judge Cole and told him the water co. wanted to retain him. He said he was not retained and could work for us . . . (He) wanted $15,000 to be our attorney for three years. I told him 'no.'

"Then he asked what I would give. I told him about $1,000. He said, 'you want me to control that committee report and have it favorable to the water co.?' I said 'yes'. He will undertake it and will come to see me as soon as he has had a meeting of the committee."

On December 6, Hubbell reported, Cole "came to see me today and wanted $5,000. I told him 'no', that $1,000 was all I would give. He promised to come back." The diary does not report on how the discussion finally was settled. Cole, however, did do some work for the Des Moines Water Company. It is a safe assumption that his final fee was nearer Hubbell's figure than his own proposition.

It was a matter of principle with Fred to pay only what he thought he owed in a business deal, and no more. On June 29, 1889, he got into a hot argument with R. T. Wellslager, an early Des Moines business-man, over a $10,000 note. At issue in the dispute was $21.33. The diary says: "Wellslager came into my office this morning about 11 o'clock and presented for payment my note of $10,000 and coupon of $300. He demanded $10,383.33. I told him there was not that much due. I figured it up and told him that I would pay $10,362.

"Then (I) drew a check for that amount. He said he would not accept that amount and started off, leaving my office at 11:16. I finished my check and started after him at 11:17. I got to the bank at 11:19. Was ready to make tender at 11:21½. Made tender to Newell . . . at 11:22.

"Newell would not take it. Wellslager came in at 11:26. I then told him I was going back to my office and tender the money again to him there. I left the bank at 11:35 and came direct to my office with the money, $10,362 in gold. Wellslager came in again at 11:44 and demanded $10,383.33. I declined and im-

H. DeVere Thompson, long-time associate of F. M.
Hubbell. Thompson and Hubbell married sisters.

Walnut Street looking east from Fifth Street in the last century

mediately tendered him $300 to settle the coupon and $10,062 to settle the note. He refused and went off. He had the note and coupon with him the second time he was in."

Hubbell was calm about that dispute. He didn't take the trouble in later diary entries to report how much he finally paid Wellslager. It would have been surprising, however, if Hubbell had given in. Incidentally, lugging $10,362 in gold from the bank to his office was quite a little chore in itself. That much gold in those days weighed upwards of 30 pounds.

Speaking of money, the Hubbell diaries give a little insight into the job (and income) of a Des Moines stenographer 66 years ago. On November 21, 1888, Hubbell wrote: "Miss Barger commenced stenography about 6 weeks ago. Lehman has paid ten dollars. I have paid 20 dollars. Six weeks at $5 per week is $30. I promised Miss Barger $4 per week every Wednesday morning until January 1, 1889. I paid her today $4 and she promised not to come again until two weeks."

Hubbell used his diaries to record expenses which he felt should be paid by one of his companies. The diary is filled with entries such as this one of April 6, 1889: "Water co. owes me expense to Cleveland. $28.75"

The diary also shows that Hubbell wanted to be certain that anything he bought was exactly as represented. On November 11, 1910, appears this statement: "I hereby guarantee that the Atlas of the World sold to F. M. Hubbell this day shall be satisfactory in every respect." The statement was signed by one C. F. Coulter, who had sold him the Atlas.

While Hubbell was exercising extreme care in the expenditure of a few dollars for an atlas, he listed these donations in the back end of his 1910 diary: "Methodist hospital $1,000, YMCA $3,000, YWCA $3,000, Drake Med. School $5,000, Home for Aged $25,000, Coliseum rents $25,000, Coliseum stock $20,-000, Greater Des Moines Committee $18,000, Red Oak road $10,000, Drake University $2,500, Roadside Settlement $1,000, Des Moines College $500, St. Mark's Memorial $1,000, Craftsman's School $2,500." The total of all these figures is $117,000. The list obviously covers gifts made over a period of several years.

Meanwhile, he was quietly generous with small acts of charity. On December 5, 1910, he took "Abbie Bechtel to Mrs. Sommer's to be taken care of at $2 per day." Ten days later he called and "found Abbie feeling well. She wants to go back to her own home next Monday. I offered her my car but she prefers the streetcar. I paid Mrs. Sommers $28 for taking care of Abbie for two weeks ending next Monday."

On June 26, 1912, Hubbell gave his note to Drake University "due in 3 years for $5,000 without interest." That appears to have been his way of making a delayed donation to the university. By way of contrast, he was still being careful of small amounts of money. On March 7, 1913, he took dinner with W. F. Mitchell at the Des Moines Club. Mitchell was Des Moines Streets Superintendent. Hubbell wrote two sentences in his diary about that dinner. One sentence said "And he paid for the dinner." That sentence was scratched out. The other sentence said, "I paid 60 cents." That was not scratched out. In other words, Hubbell paid for his own dinner.

On January 2, 1915, he heard a woman lecturer talk about the plight of the Belgians. (Belgium had been invaded by the Germans.) "I gave her $20 (for the Belgians)," the diary says.

A number of small transactions are recorded in the diaries of his later years. Such as: "Mrs. Bolander came in this morning in great distress and I loaned her $302.50 to be paid back at $50 per month. She gave us a chattel mortgage. I fear she will not be able to pay it back to us. It is a case of charity . . .

"Loaned to Mrs. Lawson $389 to pay her taxes. She is to pay in 60 days. I hope she will but some of us doubt it . . . Dinner at the Des Moines Club . . . Gave William Wilson, a poor paralytic $5."

Returning to the larger transactions again, his will directed that $20,000 be paid to the Home for the Aged after his death and $10,000 to Drake University for scholarships.

What does this all add up to: Was he a tightwad? Not really. He was personally thrifty. And he was a tough adversary in a business deal. But a tightwad never dispenses charity in large and small amounts as he did. Nor does a tightwad make such major contributions to civic projects.

Hubbell could be droll about his reputation for thrift. He spoke at a big Equitable meeting in 1914. "When I first came to Des Moines, I had a nickel in my pocket," he said. He patted his pocket and added: "I've got it there yet." That brought down the house.

In the 1920's, when Hubbell was seriously ill, the family often sent for a barber to come to Terrace Hill to shave F.M. The barber usually was Harry Brown or the late Roy Watkins.

Brown shaved Hubbell several dozen times, maybe 50 times, during one siege of illness. The barber charged $1 a shave. Hubbell paid it but he grumbled about that "high-priced barber." "When I first came here you could get a shave for 10 cents," Hubbell told Brown. Later, the family sent Brown a check for an additional amount for those services. Brown still is barbering in Des Moines.

Near the end of his life Hubbell changed his mind about the state of being poor in the 1850's as compared with poverty in the 1920's. He decided that it was better to have been poor in the pioneer days.

"The things we bought then were cheaper," he commented in 1926. "There were fewer things to buy and things offered for sale were not displayed so temptingly as they are today. Nowadays merchants lure the eye and we are tempted to buy many things we can not afford and which we do not need. Seventy years ago, we could not buy an automobile, talking machines or radios. Today the poor man often has all of these. Living expenses, rent and clothing prices were immeasurably lower then than they are today."

And in the "today" of 1955, the "poor man" of Iowa has vastly more than he had in 1926. In fact, there are very few "poor men" now, of the type Hubbell knew 100 years ago. How amazed he would have been at our airplane-television-atomic-neon light civilization of today!

12

The Equitable

AN AGENT FOR the Mutual Life Insurance Company of New York called on Fred Hubbell in Des Moines in 1865. He sold Hubbell a $3,000 policy.

Hubbell asked many questions, as might have been expected. He wanted to know about the company, "whether it would be there to pay my loss when I died, which I supposed would be in the course of 50 or 60 years." (He lived 65 more years.) He wanted to know about life insurance in general. The agent, Matthew S. Dickinson, finally lent him a book on the subject.

Hubbell immediately saw some money-making possibilities. He noted that insurance companies were required to earn only 4 per cent interest on their reserves for policy-holders.

"The legal rate of interest in Iowa was 10 per cent at that time, which easily could be obtained," he recalled in 1907. "I reasoned that a life insurance company that was only required to earn 4 per cent could gain a very large profit by loaning its reserve at 10 per cent and upward."

There was little or no insurance money available for loans in Iowa. At that time, life insurance companies in New York were prevented by law from making loans more than 50 miles from that city. Why not start an insurance company in Des Moines? Hubbell outlined the prospects to Phineas M. Casady.

"Go to it," Casady advised. Hubbell started organizing a company in 1866. He sold stock. The original sale seems to have been disappointing.

"We got only $25,000 sold," he recalled later. He called a meeting of leading Des Moines citizens. The result of that meeting is briefly recorded as follows in Hubbell's diary: "January 25, 1867—Equitable Life Insurance Company of Iowa commenced business."

Since the company was his idea, Hubbell probably could have headed the Equitable from the first. He decided that would be unwise. "As I was a boy at the time," he said in 1924, "I thought it would not do for me to be president. I must have some man of mature years. I asked Mr. Casady to be president and he said he would, so we elected him president." Hubbell was 28 years old.

To the best of Hubbell's recollection, it was Casady who named the company. "He was trying to honor the name of the old Equitable of London, now more than 150 years old," Hubbell said in a 1907 speech. "The Equitable (of Iowa) has always tried to live up to the reputation that its name suggests."

Hubbell and Casady were instructed to prepare articles of incorporation for the Iowa company. The first policy, for $2,000, was issued to Hubbell. Fred was elected secretary. Wesley Redhead was named vice president; B. F. Allen, treasurer; and Hoyt Sherman, actuary.

Thus was Iowa's first life insurance company born.

The Equitable opened its office in a few rooms on the first floor of the old Hoyt Sherman block at the northeast corner of Court Avenue and Third Street. The City Library was on the second floor.

In 1868, the Equitable had $427,000 insurance in force and $126,946 in assets. The company had fewer than 1,000 policyholders. Today the Equitable has in excess of 1 and ⅓ billion dollars of insurance in force. Assets total nearly 550 million dollars. There are 300,000 policyholders over the nation. Most of them live in northern United States.

In volume of assets, the Equitable ranks 25th among the 700 life insurance companies in the nation. No company is more strongly entrenched, or more carefully managed.

The Equitable Building in downtown Des Moines is an Iowa landmark. The structure was the highest office building west of the Mississippi River at the time it first was occupied in 1924. The 18-story building is topped by a 90-foot tower. The distance from the street to the top of the tower is 319 feet.

1867—1880 1880—1891

1891—1907 1907—1924

Early home offices of the Equitable Life Insurance Company of Iowa.

Present home office of the Equitable Life Insurance Company of Iowa.

During the first 21 years of the company's existence, Hubbell was an officer part of the time and a director all the time. Others served as company president in this period. Casady was president from 1867 to 1871, Allen in 1872 and 1873, and Hoyt Sherman from 1874 to 1887. In 1888, Hubbell was elected president. He served until 1907 when he became chairman of the board.

Meanwhile, year after year, he bought all the Equitable stock he could find. On January 1, 1888, when he was settling accounts with Jefferson S. Polk, Hubbell wrote in his diary: "I agreed with Polk on the purchase of his Equitable stock at par."

The diary for the next day says: "I took Polk's Equitable stock at par, $36,100. Paid him Equitable block $14,000, my notes 10 years, 22,000, and I owe him $100. Total $36,100. Polk will advise Sherman to sell me all his Equitable stock."

Hoyt Sherman, who was retiring as company president, owned quite a block of stock. A tabulation early in 1888 showed the Equitable stock distribution to be: Polk & Hubbell $11,100; Hoyt Sherman, $20,500; R. L. Tidrick, $2,100; H. D. Booge, $56,100; F. M. Hubbell, $6,000; A. Morris estate, $4,000, and Hamilton and Talbott, $200.

Hubbell appears in this tabulation to have been only a minor stockholder. Actually, he probably already controlled the company. More than half the outstanding stock was in the name of H. D. Booge. Booge was a brother of James E. Booge, Sioux City packer. James was the husband of Annie Hubbell, Fred's sister. She had died in 1864. Hubbell and the Booges remained close friends all their lives. It may well be that the $36,100 Equitable stock that Hubbell bought from Polk was registered in Booge's name.

The Booge holdings, Hubbell's own $6,000 and his share of Polk & Hubbell's $11,100 apparently gave Fred control of well over 50 per cent of the outstanding stock.

Be that as it may, Hoyt Sherman and Polk both had sold out and were absent from the list of Equitable stockholders by 1896. In all probability Hubbell was the buyer. Of the 4,800 shares outstanding in 1896, Hubbell personally held 949 and his cousin, Isaac W. Birdseye, owned 1,440. An "F. Burritt" was listed as holding 1,244 shares. That may have been the estate of Fred's father, Francis Burritt Hubbell, who died in 1891. If so, then Hubbell controlled 3,633 shares, or about 75 per cent of the outstanding stock.

Fred finally achieved his goal of purchasing all the issued Equitable stock. Today the company is owned in its entirety by the Hubbell interests.

The Equitable, which is the second largest life insurance company in insurance-minded Iowa, is credited with having made a vital contribution to this state's laws. The company was only a little over a year old in

the winter of 1868. Equitable officials that year success-
fully sponsored passage of Iowa's widely known insurance deposit reserve law.

Under that state statute, an insurance company
must deposit with the state insurance commissioner
interest-bearing securities equal in value to the full
amount of the company's reserve on all contracts and
policies in force. The securities must be approved by
the commissioner. At this moment, the Iowa state insurance department has nearly one billion 500 million
dollars in such securities on deposit in the state office
building for the protection of insurance policyholders.
This protection all dates back to the drive sponsored by
Equitable officials in the Iowa legislature of 1868.

Numerous comments on the Equitable appear on
the Hubbell diaries as the 19th century came to an end
and the 20th century dawned. In his own terse way,
Hubbell expressed satisfaction in the following January 2, 1900 entry: "Estimated mortality $109,000,
actual experience $53,000." The entry means that the
company had had to pay out less than half as much
money in death claims in 1899 as had been expected.

Other businessmen saw the growth of the Equitable and wanted in. On September 1, 1901, a Theodore
K. Long "wanted to buy Equitable stock." Hubbell
would not sell. "Then he wanted an option which I
refused," the diary says.

A significant statement appears under date of February 28, 1905. "Fred (F. C. Hubbell) and I further considered a railroad project and whether it would not be better to push insurance matters," the elder Hubbell wrote. "(I had) a long talk with Fred about the propriety of dropping railroad business and confining ourselves entirely to life insurance."

In the end, the Hubbells did get out of railroading and they did concentrate to an increasing degree on life insurance. F. C. Hubbell became Equitable president in 1917 and served in that capacity until 1921. He was succeeded by Henry S. Nollen, who was president from 1921 to 1939. Frederick W. Hubbell has been president since 1939. He is a son of F. C. Hubbell and a grandson of F. M. Hubbell.

Frederick W. Hubbell's entire business life has been devoted to the Equitable. He is the oldest employee of the company in years of service. He will observe his 42nd anniversary with the Equitable August 1, 1955. The company has prospered under his leadership far beyond the hopes and expectations of F. M. Hubbell.

F. W. received national recognition in the insurance field in 1954 when he was elected president of the Life Insurance Institute.

The records over the years tell the story of the Equitable's growth. On March 12, 1912, the elder Hubbell reported that "The Equitable has written one million six thousand up to this PM for March. We hope to write this month one million two hundred thousand dollars." Now, in 1955, the company shows an average increase of insurance in force of more than five million dollars a month, or more than 60 million dollars a year.

January 1, 1916, was quite an occasion for Frederick M. Hubbell and the Equitable. Here is what he wrote in his diary: "Equitable gave banquet at Des Moines Club for its agents. F.W.H. was toastmaster. I was honorary toastmaster and was presented with a goldheaded cane engraved 100,000,000." The Equitable had reached its pre-World War I goal of 100 million dollars of insurance in force. That goal has been left far behind in recent years. Here is a table showing how the company has grown since 1868:

Year	Assets	Insurance in Force
1868	$ 126,946	$ 427,200
1888	664,555	2,250,415
1893	996,669	5,512,964
1898	1,809,117	10,091,915
1903	3,616,639	21,148,031
1913	14,119,378	77,367,095
1918	25,022,114	159,618,090
1923	51,704,266	348,767,229
1933	132,000,884	569,000,000
1943	255,957,960	658,929,000
1953	505,859,279	1,300,834,807
1954	534,584,915	1,362,953,372

The company's expansion since the end of World War II in 1945 has been phenomenal. Insurance in force has increased more than 80 per cent in that 9-year period.

Few stock insurance companies devote so small a part of their earnings to profits. In 1953, for example, the Equitable's total earnings for the year were $7,144,-989. Of this amount, $4,510,000 was credited to policyholders as dividends. Surplus was increased $1,569,605 and $965,574 was used for "reserve strengthening and adjustment of assets." Only $100,000 was distributed as dividends to stockholders. The company's total surplus rose to more than 22 million dollars.

State Insurance Commissioner Charles R. Fischer says the Equitable "is one of the finest companies in the United States."

— 13 —

Health

IT WAS NO happenstance that Fred Hubbell lived more than 91 years. He prized his health and he guarded it carefully.

As a youth, Hubbell had an idea that he would die young. He believed he inherited a condition from his mother that would take him early. (She died at 45.) Fred did not record what was wrong with his mother.

When he was 19 years old, and still at Sioux City, he wrote: "If God will give me health until I am 40 years of age, I am confident that I can win a respectable if not honorable name in society and the nation."

Yet, he was rugged physically until he got old. He had a marvelous constitution. His teeth were remarkably good. He had all but one of his teeth until he was 79 years old.

Hubbell always seemed to have an absorbing interest in death. Whenever a friend or associate died, he recorded that fact in his diary. Sometimes twice. He reported the death of Hoyt Sherman January 25, 1904, in both the annual diary and the "perpetual" one.

125

Sherman was 76 years 2 months and 24 days old at time of death.

Hubbell was 65 years old when Sherman died. You get the impression that every time Hubbell wrote down a person's age at death he subconsciously calculated how much of his own life was left. It was as if he said to himself on January 25, 1904: "Hoyt died at 76. I am 65. Therefore, I guess I am pretty certain to live 10 more years."

Hubbell did a strange thing in 1915 and 1916. He clipped a number of obituaries from the New York Post and recorded how long the various deceased persons had lived. Hubbell was 76 years old in 1915. He found that the Post on June 12, 1915, reported the deaths of 10 persons under 76 years of age. Younger than he was, in other words.

On October 19, there were obituaries in the Post of 14 persons who were less than 76 years old. On December 14, there were six such deaths reported. Hubbell's own life span had exceeded theirs.

At the back end of the "perpetual" diary are two pages headed: "Names of some of my contemporaries." There Hubbell listed names, dates of birth, dates of death and ages at death, as follows:

"Name	Date of Birth	Date of Death	Yrs.	Mos.	Days
"Isaac Cooper	Feb. 8, 1813	Aug. 13, 1902	89	6	5

"Francis B.

Hubbell ...Mar. 27, 1814   Nov. 29, 1890   76   8   2
"P. M.

Casady ....Dec. 3, 1818   Aug. 31, 1908   89   8   28"

And so on. There are 58 names on the list. All were not Des Moines or Iowa persons by any means. For example, he reported that "Hill, James J." lived for 77 years, 8 months and 13 days. Hill was a noted railroad baron in St. Paul. He built the Great Northern. Also, Hubbell reported in this list that Admiral George Dewey, hero of Manila Bay in the Spanish-American war, lived for 79 years, no months and 20 days.

Only once was he injured to any substantial extent. On December 6, 1886, Polk said in a letter to Grenville Dodge: "Mr. Hubbell has been confined to his bed for seven weeks. The night you left your car in Des Moines he sprained his ankle when he got off the car and that brought on an attack of rheumatism and he has been a very great sufferer since that time, having had several severe operations performed on the ankle. He is improving but the improving is slow and may take some time yet before he entirely recovers."

There isn't a word about that difficulty anywhere in the surviving Hubbell papers. Incidentally, it should be pointed out that he was no hypochondriac. He was much too active and healthy a man for that. He paid considerable attention to his well being because health to him was an important asset. Hubbell never was careless with any of his assets.

Impressed with Hubbell's good health in his old age, one historian wrote in 1915: "Although past the 76th milestone on life's journey, he (Hubbell) possesses the vigor, energy and determination of a man 25 years his junior."

Fred's penchant for keeping records extended to his own weight. "Was weighed today after Turkish bath," he wrote October 10, 1901. "135½." His weight over the diary years varied from 119 to 147 pounds.

He ate little, purposely, especially in his later years. At 86, he said he hadn't had a headache in 30 years. "I went to Dr. Smouse 29 years ago," he recalled. "The doctor told me the best sort of diet was to eat two meals a day, breakfast and dinner. He didn't charge me a cent but it has been worth thousands to me, and has added many years to my life. I had been eating too much. Most people do but don't know it."

He ate breakfast at 8 and dinner at 4. "If I eat three meals, my disposition suffers," he said. In 1927 he told a reporter: "I turned over a new leaf at dinner. I did not eat until I was full. I don't think I ate more than two-thirds as much as I usually do."

Hubbell constantly worried about "catching something." "Got a sore throat by walking from the east front door to the auto without protecting my throat," he wrote February 12, 1911. "Sent for Dr. Moore at 8 p.m."

He drank practically no liquor except on doctor's orders. In 1903 he went through a serious siege of pneumonia. He was down for weeks. His physician sent him to Florida to recuperate. On medical advice, he took "whisky before breakfast" for two days. He got well.

He was grateful to that physician for the rest of his life. Hubbell often said the doctor had saved his life. In later years, when the physician was having his troubles around Des Moines, the Hubbells rented him office space in recognition of the elder Hubbell's gratitude.

On another occasion in his old age, Hubbell walked out on the porch of his home after a period of illness. He wrote: "As I stepped out, I exclaimed, 'thank God I am outdoors once more.' I was so overcome I burst into tears."

The diary is sprinkled with little observations having to do with the life of a man getting on in years. In 1901, he drolly reported going to a doctor in Chicago. The doctor gave him some capsules, told Hubbell "to stay away as long as I could and send him $25." On March 5, 1905, he was sick again and his family sent for Dr. Edmundsen. The diary says the doctor "rubbed my chest $3 worth."

On July 15, 1907, Hubbell began using a substance "on the spot on my face today. Recommended by Frank Allen the barber." Evidently the stuff worked. The "spot" caused no further trouble. On October 1, 1909, Hubbell wrote that he had "a queer feeling in my right forefinger." That feeling also apparently disappeared.

Despite all his concern with diet, he occasionally yielded to temptation and ate more than he should have. During some railroad negotiations in Texas in 1904, he wrote:

"Dinner, soup, turkey, cranberry, potatoes, almonds, tomatoes, strawberry, claret, champagne, cigar.

"Sick, sick, sick."

14

Family

THE POSSESSIVE INSTINCTS of Fred Hubbell extended to people. He treasured his business associates and friends. Most of all, he treasured his family, even remote members of it.

Nothing delighted him so much as to do something for a Hubbell, or a Hubbell in-law. "They're all mine, these human beings," he seemed to say to himself. "They belong to Frederick M. Hubbell, the boy from the Connecticut neighborhood where everybody talked about going to the poorhouse."

The Hubbell diaries are rich in items of family joy and sorrow, pride and crisis, anxiety and achievement. As far back as 1858, when things were tough for 19-year-old Hubbell in Sioux City, he once wrote: "Got a letter from Annie today. I wish I was able to pay for her education. Music and all. She is improving in her letter writing very much." (Annie was his 15-year-old sister, back in Huntington, Conn.)

The later diaries are often filled with personal references to his children, particularly his son Grover and his daughter Beulah. The oldest son, Fred Cooper

131

Hubbell, was born in 1864. He was 17 and pretty well grown up when the annual diaries were resumed in 1881. Thus, most of the diary comments on Fred C. concern business problems.

Grover was born February 3, 1883. The proud father had the boy's physical measurements taken each year. January 2, 1899, when Grover was 15 years old, the diary carries this information: "Grover's measurements. Height 4 ft. 11½ in. across shoulders 15 in. chest 29 in. waist 26½ in. thigh higher part 16½ in. thigh lower part 11 in. calf 12 in. arm high part 8½ in. lower part 8½ in."

When Grover arrived, his father let railroads, insurance, waterworks and real estate go hang for a few days. The only entry in the diary for February 4, 1883, is: "Stayed home all day and took care of wife and baby." On October 18, of that year, the diary reports: "Weaned the baby today."

Grover went away to school for the first time in 1898. The diary for September 15 and 16, of that year says: "Started with Grover to Culver, Ind. (military academy) . . . Paid for Grover's tuition. First term $200. Athletic association and entertainment fund $10. Tuition $50, suits of clothes $65. Pocket money, books and incidentals, $25. $350 (total). He takes Latin, algebra, Greek, ancient history, rhetoric and cavalry. Started home today at noon."

Grover later attended a prep school at Lawrenceville, N. J. One day a circular arrived at the Hubbell home from Lawrenceville. The circular said a certain boy identified only by the alias of "Halsey" was in danger of flunking physics. Fred Hubbell had a suspicion. He sent this telegram to the Lawrenceville headmaster: "Who is Halsey named in circular you sent me? My boy's name is Grover. Is Grover doing passing work?"

Back came this answer: "Grover's condition in physics serious. Like condition in French and algebra."

The astonished father couldn't believe it. A son of Fred Hubbell having trouble in school? Fred Hubbell, who had needed no teacher to help him study Latin, law, trigonometry and shorthand? He sent a letter to Grover immediately.

"I hope you will study nights, take extra lessons or employ someone to teach you out of school hours," the father wrote. "I do not want you to drop behind in physics. I do not know what physics is but suppose it is natural philosophy, a study I was very fond of, and I see no reason why you should be deficient in it . . . Don't fail in physics, algebra or French. Work nights, work Sundays, work all the time and don't get behind in any of your classes."

Grover got through Lawrenceville all right. Yale was next. On February 2, 1904, the diary says: "Wrote

Grover. Asked him to promise me not to smoke or drink until after he finishes college."

The April 16, 1904, diary reports that Grover had passed all his examinations. The diary adds: "He (Grover) is in high spirits and has everything he wants except a wife and an automobile. He may want more later on. These two things are uppermost in his mind now."

Grover certainly had a tough schedule at Yale. The diary for September 17, 1904, says: "Grover's studies are French, German, calculus, differential and integral, bridge drafting, railroad engineering, masonry construction, English." He passed all his courses, however, and received an engineering degree at Yale.

Grover had considerable difficulty with his health over a period of several years. On June 13, 1918, he went to Los Alamos ranch in New Mexico (near where they now manufacture fissionable atomic materials). Grover and his family remained in New Mexico for two years and three months, or until September 10, 1920. The diary reflects the father's anxiety over his son's condition and, eventually, relief over Grover's recovery.

His daughter, Beulah, also was very much on Fred Hubbell's mind down through the years. "Had a little daughter born," he reported in his perpetual diary in 1874. Her illnesses were not many. "Beulah commenced on tonic this a.m.," the diary says for August

FREDERICK C. HUBBELL

GROVER C. HUBBELL

1, 1894. That is one of the few references to her health anywhere in his papers.

Fred Hubbell wanted very much to do well by his daughter. In 1898, when she was 24 years old, he promised her an allowance of $12,000 a year. She was in Europe at the time and engaged to Count Carl Wachtmeister, a Swedish diplomat.

Was the count the man for Beulah to marry? Fred Hubbell became dubious for some reason. He resolved to go to Europe. On July 21, 1898, he sent Beulah this cable: "Don't accelerate matters. I sail on the Umbria Saturday."

On August 2, he met Beulah at Hamburg, Germany. "Had a long talk with her," he wrote in his diary. "She intends to go home with me. That much is settled, I think."

Three days later he wrote that "Beulah felt bad and made me feel very unhappy." On August 7, Hubbell sent word home that Beulah was "weak, sick, cross and that she gave me no satisfaction as to her plans . . ." On August 17, the father reported that Beulah was "all at sea about what to do matrimonially."

Hubbell finally came home alone. By the spring of 1899, Beulah decided to marry Count Wachtmeister. Father Hubbell gave the couple his blessing. On May 1, 1899, presumably as a dowry, he gave Beulah his note due in 10 years for $200,000 and paying 4 per cent interest on January 1, each year. In other words, he provided her with $8,000 annual income.

On May 2, 1899, the diary says: "Beulah Cooper Hubbell married to C. A. Wachtmeister this evening at Terrace Hill."

The diary description of the wedding is brief and terse. Yet that event was one of the most colorful ceremonies in Des Moines history. The story of the wedding is given in a later chapter of this book.

Hubbell was deeply fond of Beulah and, as it worked out, tremendously proud of Count Wachtmeister and of his Countess daughter. On December 8, 1899, Hubbell reported in his diary: "Beulah was presented at the Swedish Court today. She arrived at palace at 3:45. Tea was served at 4:15." Hubbell wasn't there personally. He relayed to the diary what Beulah had reported either in a letter or a telegram.

Fred Hubbell was always sending Beulah substantial gifts (perhaps because diplomats have to live expensive lives). On January 7, 1900, he wrote: "Sent Beulah 200 (English) pounds . . . Told her I was going to fix her up with $80,000 very soon. Will open a set of books for her and bring them to Europe for her inspection."

Count Wachtmeister was secretary of the Swedish consulate in Chicago when he met Miss Hubbell. He was 28 years old when he married Beulah. She was 25. In 1900 he was appointed attache to the Swedish legation in Paris. He was named Swedish consul general in Havana, Cuba, in 1904. The Cuban climate did not agree with Beulah. The Wachtmeisters left Havana and went on a world tour. They were in Calcutta in 1918 when the count received news of his appointment as consul general in Cairo, Egypt. The count retired from diplomatic service after the war ended and he and Beulah moved to Paris. He died in 1935.

On March 9, 1904, Hubbell met the count at New Orleans. "Glad to see him and he is looking well," Fred wrote of the count. "I agreed to make him independent by giving him $250 per month and giving Beulah $800 per month. In all each month $1,050."

The only child of the Count and Countess is Fredrik H. C. Wachtmeister. He was born April 27, 1909. Young Fredrik's name appeared in a droll August 17, 1911, entry in the Hubbell diary when the child was 2 years old. On that date, Hubbell wrote: "Nobody works but father. Fred C. Hubbell on his way to hunt moose in Alaska. Grover C. Hubbell out playing tennis. Fred W. Hubbell (grandson) in Tacoma courting Ruth Anderson. James W. Hubbell (also grandson) playing golf in Omaha. Fredrik H. C. Wachtmeister is with his mother at Terrace Hill. Not old enough to work. Two years and four months. F. M. Hubbell is on the job. Exchanged deeds with the city for vacating 6th Street south of Murphy."

The senior Hubbell apparently was worried in World War I days over the Wachtmeisters, who were in Europe most of the time. He ordinarily didn't mention historic events in his diary. But on March 28, 1918, he wrote: "This completes the first week of the German drive on Paris. Received a cablegram from Carl from Stockholm that the King had appointed him minister to Cairo." (The Wachtmeisters had gone to Stockholm after getting the news in Calcutta.)

On November 16, 1918, five days after the Armistice, Hubbell was happy to report: "Beulah and Carl arrived this morning at 7:10 a.m. Beulah looks a little thin but is well. Had a hard disagreeable voyage, 18 days on a ship from Spain to Cuba."

Even in the last years of his diary, Hubbell kept track of Beulah's travels. On February 28, 1924, when he was 85 years old, he wrote that "Beulah sailed today on the Steamship Olympia for England."

Hubbell wanted Wachtmeister to be a diplomat all his life. A Hubbell letter dated December 11, 1902, advised the count not to go into business. In the letter Hubbell said in part: "I am engaged in business and some time have to take chances and I don't want you to do the same. One of us is enough to take risks. When I am gone your income I expect will be very much inflated and you can then take the surplus or a part of it and try business if you want to, though I should not even recommend that."

COUNTESS BEULAH HUBBELL WACHTMEISTER in 1899.

TERRACE HILL

He told the count to "invest in real estate and collect the rents for an income, or when you have a surplus, learn to lend money, take security and collect the interest. If you invest in real estate," he advised Wachtmeister, "you will not lose the principal, 95% of businessmen don't succeed."

The count took his father-in-law's advice about not going into business. He remained a diplomat all his life. The countess, now 80, lives in Paris. She is an occasional visitor to Des Moines.

On May 5, 1881, Hubbell wrote in his diary: "Gave my wife diamonds this evening. $2,700." This is one of his few unworried references to Frances Cooper Hubbell, whom he married in 1863. She was a chronic sufferer from asthma and was plagued by ill health most of her life.

As early as June 1, 1870, Hubbell wrote in the big diary: "Left my wife at water cure." He evidently had taken Mrs. Hubbell to a mineral springs resort for rest and treatment. He was forever searching for someone who could provide her with relief. In his last years he wrote: "Major Walter S. Sharpe, M.D., and J.M. Rich of Fort Des Moines gave their treatment to Frances at 4 p.m. today. It was very beneficial, relieving her of asthma and nervous spasms. They will come again Sunday for another treatment."

The relief was only temporary. Mrs. Hubbell lived to an old age, however. She died at Terrace Hill May 11, 1924, at the age of 84.

After his own family had grown up, Fred Hubbell transferred much of his attention and anxiety to his grandchildren. He proudly recorded the births of all his grandchildren in his diary. Grover has three daughters. They are Frances Cooper Hubbell Ingham, born October 18, 1906; Helen Virginia Thorne Barshell, born February 12, 1908, and Mary Belle Hubbell Windsor, born December 15, 1911.

Frederick C. Hubbell's two sons are Frederick Windsor Hubbell and James Windsor Hubbell. Frederick W. was born November 24, 1891, and James W. June 5, 1895.

Among other things, the grandfather did not want the boys to smoke. On August 11, 1916, he drew up a legal "article of agreement" with James W. Hubbell, then 21 years old. The agreement in part said:

"Whereas, F. M. Hubbell is the grandfather of said James Windsor Hubbell and is animated with an earnest desire that said James shall not contract the habit of using tobacco in any form. Now therefore, it is agreed as follows, to-wit: The said James Windsor Hubbell hereby agrees that during the life-time of said F. M. Hubbell, he will not use tobacco, by smoking cigars, pipes or cigarettes, or by chewing tobacco, taking snuff or using any kind of tobacco in any other form.

"In consideration of the great sacrifice that said James Windsor Hubbell agrees to make in the foregoing paragraph, the said F. M. Hubbell agrees to pay him ONE DOLLAR per day, to be paid at the end of every month during the life of this contract. But if the said James Windsor Hubbell violates this contract by using tobacco in any form, said violation shall work as a forfeiture of the $1 per day he otherwise would have received, and shall obligate him to pay to said F. M. Hubbell $1 per day for each and every day that he, the said James Windsor Hubbell, uses tobacco in any form.

"It is understood that the money and the income therefrom, received by said James Windsor Hubbell under this contract shall be saved and invested under the supervision and approval of F. M. Hubbell or F. C. Hubbell."

It appears that the contract did not remain in force for very long. The United States had entered World War I in 1917. In 1918, F. W. Hubbell was in the army. On May 20, 1918, the elder Hubbell wrote: "Jim (J. W.) was in and wanted me to give him $200 to pay his expenses to visit F. W. Hubbell at Camp Cody. He said that when the war was over that he would give up smoking in consideration of the above sum. I paid it, trusting implicitly that he would keep his agreement in good faith."

Jim soon followed his brother into the army and on August 15, 1918, the diary says: "James W. Hubbell sailed for France today. His mother was in New York to say goodbye to him."

The war ended November 11. On December 16, the diary says: "Frederick W. Hubbell was discharged today from the U. S. Army and left for Chicago to meet his wife at the Blackstone." A week later, Captain Hubbell returned from Chicago "and went to work at the Equitable."

On June 15, 1919, the diary says that "Jim Hubbell arrived from France this evening. I went over to his father's house to meet him at dinner."

Both grandsons later were widely known Des Moines polo players. A story is told that F. M. grunted with surprise one day while checking the books in the Hubbell office.

"What's this item of $200 for shipping polo ponies to Kansas?" he wanted to know. An employee explained the grandsons had authorized the expenditure. Hubbell pointed out that his pay for a whole year's work was less than $200 when he first came to Des Moines. Then his eyes twinkled and he said to the employee:

"Don't you wish you had had a rich grandfather?"

FREDERICK W. HUBBELL

JAMES W. HUBBELL

15

The City Council

FRED HUBBELL REFUSED to touch any proposition tainted with corruption.

Late in 1888, he owned substantial interests in both the North Des Moines and Des Moines waterworks. North Des Moines was a separate municipality then.

Hubbell wanted the North Des Moines council to pass a certain ordinance. A leading Des Moines businessman called on Hubbell. The businessman reported that one councilman would vote for the ordinance in return for a $700 payoff. Another councilman wanted $500. The businessman expressed belief that the ordinance could be passed if $3,000 were distributed in the right places.

Hubbell's reaction was swift. The diary says he told the visitor: "I could not consent to having the ordinances passed by bribery and corruption and . . . if it could not be passed on its merits I would rather have it fail than have him pay councilmen for it."

Furthermore, the diary continues, Hubbell warned the visitor that he was laying himself open to a possible indictment for corruption.

143

The diary does not record whether the ordinance was passed. Probably it wasn't. The City Councils in the Des Moines area did not do Hubbell's bidding with much regularity. (Greenwood Park also had its own council in those days, and so did University Place in the Drake University neighborhood.)

Even though the Des Moines City Council thwarted him most of the time, Hubbell always gave a big dinner once a year to council members at Terrace Hill. There was nothing secret about these dinners. The whole town knew of them.

The town did not know, however, that Hubbell and his guests played poker after dinner. At the 1917 dinner, Mayor John MacVicar, Sr., won $7.95. At the 1918 dinner, Tom Fairweather lost $5; Frank Jeffries won $8.90; Lafayette Young, editor of the old Des Moines Capital, lost $4.30 and Hubbell himself won 60 cents. Hubbell reported the outcome of the games in his diary.

The council's cold attitude toward Fred stemmed from three things: (1) Hubbell was rich and it didn't pay politically to appear to be kowtowing to a rich man; (2) the city of Des Moines had been trying vainly for two generations to buy the waterworks from Hubbell and his associates, and (3) Hubbell wanted Hubbell Avenue opened in northeast Des Moines. The council was suspicious that the resourceful Hubbell had a scheme up his sleeve to make a killing from the

Hubbell Avenue project. (He didn't, or if he did, it didn't work.)

The waterworks conflict was the big battle. It lasted nearly half a century. The first Des Moines waterworks company was organized in 1871 with a capital stock of $250,000. Jefferson Polk and Fred Hubbell were key men in the company.

It was not until 1919, or 48 years later, that the city succeeded in buying the present municipal water system.

The water fight was a long and rugged struggle, interspersed with periods of comparative peace. B. F. Allen was the first waterworks president and Polk was the first secretary. Hubbell was listed as one of the incorporators. By 1875 he had become secretary of the company. By 1888, he and his lieutenants such as H. D. Thompson, Frederick C. Hubbell, Chris Huttenlocher and A. N. Denman had formed the separate Des Moines Water Supply Company. That company was started to provide water for such communities as North Des Moines, Greenwood Park and University Place.

By 1896, Hubbell was doing business as president of the Des Moines Waterworks Company. From the 1870's clear up to 1919, the Hubbell interests in the water company always were substantial.

The first Des Moines Water Company operated at a loss in its early years. For example, Hubbell as company secretary reported June 5, 1876, that the losses for a year totaled $17,487. That in part was due to the bonds outstanding. The bonds paid 10 per cent interest (a normal rate in those days). Of the company's $49,439 operating expense for the year, $24,624 was bond interest, or nearly half the total.

The city levied a two-mill property tax then for municipal water rents. That money went to the company. Householders also paid water bills. Even so, the company appeared to have lost money.

Political blowups over water were frequent in the 48-year span. Somebody always was starting a movement for the city to take over the waterworks. The company, however, had a 40-year franchise, granted in 1871.

There was hardly a dull moment in some years. On March 3, 1879, one Alderman Hammer sponsored a resolution in the city council calling the water franchise "a monstrous fraud and usurpation of power on its face . . ." He said the ordinance had been "conceived in sin and brought forth in iniquity . . ."

Moves to reduce water rates were numerous. Occasionally the rates were forced down.

There was constant talk of shutting off all the water if the franchise were canceled. The council frequently jumped on the company because the water was dirty. The company vigorously defended itself. In 1883, the franchise was canceled by a 5 to 4 vote of the council.

But the cancellation didn't stick. There were frequent public mass meetings against and for the franchise, and threats of plans to build a municipally-owned competing water system.

In 1893, the company did offer to sell the system to the city for $1,300,000. The deal fell through. In 1895, the clerks in the water company office were arrested and charged with extortion because they had been collecting rates in excess of an 1893 ordinance. (The clerks were not prosecuted. The arrests were part of the war of nerves.) Later, Charles Denman, waterworks manager, was arrested for selling "impure water."

In 1898, a proposal for the city to buy the waterworks was beaten by 188 votes in a city election. The waterworks question was on the ballot in one way or another a number of times in succeeding years.

In 1914, the voters approved purchase of the water plant and approved issuance of bonds. A second bond issue election had to be held, however, for technical reasons. The people voted down the bonds the second time. Finally, in 1919, the people approved the purchase of the water system for $3,450,000, paid for with 5 per cent bonds. The last of the bonds mature in 1969.

Incidentally, the water company was not alone in its troubles with the council and the people all those years. The streetcar company and the gas and electric utilities also were under fire much of the time.

In the long running battle of the council against the water company, some of the fire was directed at Hubbell. Much of the time, however, he was not too publicly prominent in the conflict. He was busy with his railroads, with his insurance, real estate and other interests. Nevertheless, he was very much involved in water affairs, far more sometimes than the public realized.

As early as 1881, Hubbell went out selling Des Moines water bonds around the United States. In Cleveland on January 3, of that year, he "sold water bonds to A. Stone $10,000 and ordered $32,000 more sent to him by express." On January 8, he sold $15,000 bonds to the Peoples Savings Bank in Cleveland and $17,000 more to Stone. The diary does not say whether they were his bonds, or whether he sold them for the company.

In any event, his interest in the water company was substantial enough so that he was elected director in 1883. (B. F. Kauffman was elected president.)

Hubbell kept close track of water company affairs. On February 19, 1883, he wrote: "Was out most of today testing waterworks. Nine streams on west side and six streams on east side." (One of the franchise requirements was that the waterworks equipment must have been capable of simultaneously throwing six streams of water 100 feet vertically into the air through one inch nozzles.)

By 1881, the waterworks was taking in more than $51,000 revenue a year from users. The total revenues in 1873 were $15,000. Waterworks revenue thus more than tripled in 8 years.

In 1889, Hubbell wrote: "King, Sheldon and Weitz in behalf of the city council came to see me and wanted to acquire the waterworks for the city. I told them several times that the company did not want to sell . . ."

In his diary, Hubbell once outlined the terms under which he would deal with a private buyer. "I want water free always," he wrote in 1888. "I want the right to put in stock (in the transaction) at a price up to $500,000. I want one-third of the profits on any new reorganization of works. I want the purchaser to guarantee sale of new bonds at a price not lower than 95. I want my side to have one-third of all salaries and perquisites and the right to buy new stock or bonds at the same price as sold to others and to take one-third thereof at my option. I want contract to protect me so they will have to make me an offer to give or take whenever I want them to. I want contract to light my house. I want $10,000 of second mortgage bonds and all of my floating debts taken care of."

This list of requirements probably is of historical interest even though there is no open record of any buyer having dealt with him on that basis. Yet, he did sell part of his waterworks holdings in 1895. He announced on November 5, that year that he had sold his stock in the water company to C. F. Parks of Boston, Mass. Hubbell was company president at the time.

At the same time, he either retained a sizable interest in waterworks bonds, or he later regained part of his former holdings. In the 1895 sale, he might well have insisted on part of the 1888 terms.

Back in the 1880s, Hubbell did a lot of buying and selling of water stock around Des Moines. On May 25, 1888, for example, he wrote: "I asked Oliver Perkins, H. K. Love and J. H. Windsor for an option on their water stock at 35. Told them I was going to sell out the controlling interest." (Which he did, but not until 7 years later.)

The next day, Hubbell asked Ben Kauffman for an option on his water stock at 35. Kauffman "offered to give it to me at 40 and I took it." He also got Oliver Perkins' stock the same day for $35 a share. A few days later he procured an option on J. H. Windsor's 230 shares at $35.

That Windsor deal started a minor revolution. On August 11, 1888, Hubbell wrote: "Had a talk with Windsor in my office. He said that as I had not sold the works he did not want his stock to go out but wanted it back. I told him I would think about it . . ."

The more Windsor thought, the madder he got. On August 24, Hubbell sent DeVere Thompson over to talk with Windsor. "Windsor was wild and crazy with his grievances and refused my check of $8,050," the diary says. "I employed Kauffman and Guernsey to make the tender."

The next day, Attorney Guernsey "took my check and tendered it to Windsor who refused. I then gave Guernsey $8,050 in gold and DeVere and Guernsey took a horse and buggy and started for Windsor's park house," the diary reports. "They met him and had a lively chase but overtook him and made the tender, which he refused."

The argument had died down two days later. Hubbell wrote on August 27, that "Windsor accepted my check today for his stock."

Hubbell and Windsor later were close friends. Windsor's daughter Mary was the wife of Frederick C. Hubbell. She was the mother of the present Frederick Windsor Hubbell and James Windsor Hubbell.

Meanwhile, Hubbell kept pegging away before the turn of the century, trying to obtain water franchises in the Des Moines area. He brushed off one defeat after another. On October 19, 1888, he tersely reported: "Went to North Des Moines with Macy and Denman to the council. Our ordinance was voted down, five against to two for it." But by November 20, the deal was completed to buy the North Des Moines works for $55,000. Wrote Hubbell: "Paid money and notes and took the N. Des Moines water company away with us."

It is interesting to note that Hubbell in 1896 still had plenty to say about the operations of the Des Moines Waterworks, even though he had sold his stock the year before. On May 1, of that year, he was somewhat worried about the salary of Augustus Denman, the manager. Hubbell wrote: "Talked to Denman about his salary. He said he was not asking a raise and I told him the finances of the company would not permit a large salary this year."

The next day, Denman told Hubbell that "he thought it not necessary" to reduce his salary. The diary doesn't disclose whether the salary went up or down, or just stayed put.

In 1919, when negotiations for sale of the waterworks to the city were going strong, the elder Hubbell got into trouble with one of his sons, Fred C. Hubbell. The diary for March 21, says: "FCH came to my office this PM and gave me an awful scolding because I told the reporter that I was going to vote for the purchase of the waterworks and that they were worth a million dollars more than the city was paying for them." The son evidently thought it unwise for the elder Hubbell to be quoted at that time.

Hubbell's comment in the newspapers did not stir up any resentment, however. The water plant election brought out a very light vote, considering the length and heat of the 48-year controversy. The "yes" vote was 2,744, the "noes" numbered 1,885.

There is no question but that an eastern syndicate headed by C. H. Payson of Portland, Maine, held a majority interest in the Des Moines Waterworks at the time of final sale. But Hubbells had an important interest also. How the $3,450,000 received from the city was distributed among the former owners never was officially disclosed. But present day estimates indicate the Hubbell interests owned perhaps a third of the waterworks company at the time of the 1919 sale.

The North Des Moines Waterworks bribery offer probably was only one of many that Hubbell squelched in his lifetime. His diary mentions other similar instances.

Back in 1906, Fifth Street in Des Moines was not open between Grand and what is now Keo. Hubbell had some property in that vicinity. (Indeed, the Insurance Exchange Building at Fifth and Grand is located on land still owned by Trustees of the Frederick M. Hubbell Estate and F. M. Hubbell, Son & Company, Incorporated.)

Hubbell was anxious to have Fifth Street opened. On March 30, a Des Moines city alderman came to see him. The alderman said he had been told he could get $300 for voting for Fifth Street.

"I told him (the alderman) that I had no right to promise money," the diary says, "that if it could not go through on its own merits I wanted it defeated, that I would not pay anything for it. He went away and I called up Mr. Cohen and told him not to draw the contract, that I wanted to withdraw the proposition."

Hubbell's attitude apparently alarmed city officials. Several came to see him. He told them he hoped the Fifth Street project would not pass.

Two months later, however, he was interested again in opening the street. In fact, he was willing to pay $1,000 to J. A. Harding to handle the drive to get the street open. Harding was a Des Moines realtor. Hubbell was willing to pay attorney and professional fees to promote his projects. But he was dead set against allowing graft to enter the picture.

Fifth Street finally was opened in 1917.

Hubbell, of course, was fair game for candidates who wanted money with which to finance city election campaigns. Back in 1897, he told J. C. Macy that he "would contribute $25 to $50 for his nomination as councilman next spring." Macy did serve on the council.

In 1912, Zell Roe wanted to be a candidate for city office. He called up Hubbell. The diary says: "He (Roe) said he should be a candidate either for mayor or councilman next spring and would have two other men run with him and propose to control the council.

That he had been at work some time laying plans and lining up his forces and would have most all the Union labor vote . . . He wanted me to put in $2,500 to his campaign and that I should have everything I wanted for the next two years as he would be in control. I told him I would think it over. He wanted me to let him know this week but I told him I could not decide until next week. I agreed that our talk should be confidential."

Roe ran for the council and was elected. The diary two years later discloses that Hubbell did contribute to Roe's campaign fund, but not nearly as substantially as Roe had suggested. The diary on January 23, 1914, says: "I sent for Zell Roe this AM, told him that I appreciated the help he had given me on the ordinance widening Grand Avenue between Fourteenth and Fifteenth and that I wanted to contribute towards the campaign fund. He did not want to take anything now but would see me next Tuesday." Hubbell, however, was not altogether happy with Roe's actions as a councilman in the preceding two years. The diary says: "I told him that we put $250 into his campaign two years ago and that he voted to make us pay $90,000 for a viaduct over the Coon River on Seventh Street and that our lawyers charged us an $800 fee."

The diary for "next Tuesday" does not say whether Hubbell contributed anything toward Roe's 1914 campaign fund.

Hubbell contributed to many candidates for city office. Sometimes they won. Nevertheless, he was thwarted more often than not when matters affecting his interest came up before the council.

Probably Hubbell's most frustrating experiences with the council stemmed from the street that bears his name. Hubbell wanted the city to build a diagonal main thoroughfare from East Grand Avenue to the northeast city limits. As early as 1883 he expressed interest in such a street. Not until 1922, or 39 years later, did the council pass the resolution to open Avenue Frederick M. Hubbell, which starts at East Eighteenth and Grand.

Hubbell spent an estimated $95,000 of his own money in procuring right-of-way and in other expenses of the new avenue. A newspaper story of the times said: "He gave to the city in 1910 a strip of land through his holdings in east Des Moines, seeking the establishment by the city council of a direct road from Grand Avenue . . ."

He persuaded many small property holders along the proposed route to give part of their land for right-of-way. What he could not induce the owners to donate, he bought himself and presented the real estate to the city. He told the council: "Such roads radiating from the business district would save thousands of miles of travel and thousands of years of time."

After his retirement, he often expressed pride in his successful promotion of the Avenue. Commenting on the time the Avenue saved travelers coming into Des Moines from the northeast, he once said: "As long as they don't spend those extra hours wastefully, I am glad they have the road."

At his request, the route was named Avenue Frederick M. Hubbell. That name is the longest of any street in the city.

In 1909, the diary called the project "Northeast Boulevard." At that time, Hubbell offered A. B. Elliott $500 if he could get right-of-way cleared for the avenue. Hubbell also said he would give $200 an acre for all right-of-way "that we could not get donated."

In 1910, Hubbell talked with Mayor Hanna about the proposed street. "He (Hanna) was unwilling to vote for it," Hubbell reported. "Wanted time to look into it." The councilmen were reluctant also. Hubbell went to a council meeting and asked approval of a resolution by the city to accept 15 deeds of property for the avenue project. Not one councilman would vote for the resolution.

May 6, 1915, Hubbell called on "Alderman Mitchell". "Told him (Mitchell) that I wanted to deed to the city a 70-foot street from Eighteenth and Grand to Twenty-fifth and Easton Blvd." the diary says. Hubbell's offer was not accepted at the time. The fight was destined to last seven years longer. It was not until

August 31, 1922, that he was able to write in his diary: "I attended city council meeting to see that the resolution to open Avenue Frederick M. Hubbell was passed. They kept me there till 11:30 but they finally passed by three votes. MacVicar voted no."

Why was the council so hard-nosed about approving Hubbell Avenue? Ire over the waterworks may have been one reason. Possibly more important was the suspicion that Hubbell somehow was going to make a lot of money out of the proposed street. He owned considerable property along East Grand Avenue and in Northeast Des Moines.

If Hubbell anticipated a major real estate boom in that area, he was disappointed. No big expansion of real estate values came to pass. His thinking, however, was much broader than day-by-day real estate prices in one section of the city. His major purpose in promoting the street might be stated this way: "What's good for Des Moines is good for me."

In his younger days, Hubbell had promoted and helped build a number of narrow gauge railroads leading into Des Moines. His theory was that such roads would help Des Moines grow. He wanted diagonal access streets and roads built in Des Moines for the same reason. Regarding Hubbell Avenue, a later news story said: "He (Hubbell) sought extension of the northeast highway to Marshalltown along the Great Western tracks. It became his great ambition to see the road completed to Marshalltown before he died."

Death came in 1930. Not until six years later was Highway 64, the northeast diagonal highway, completed to Marshalltown.

Once Hubbell Avenue was completed in Des Moines, he drew considerable praise from Des Moines leaders. The Des Moines Tribune said in 1925: "Mr. Hubbell has done a service to the city that will be more fully appreciated as time passes, one that nobody but himself would have thought of doing and that nobody but himself would have done."

16

The Hubbell Estate

WEALTH IS NOT immortal. A fortune founded by one man is likely to melt away in the generations of his children and grandchildren. The old adage says: "Three generations from shirt sleeves to shirt sleeves."

Fred Hubbell was determined that his family would not go through such an evolution. "There will be none of that in the Hubbell family," he once said. "I've taken care of that."

Shortly after 1900, Hubbell discussed with Frederick C., his son, what should be done about preserving the family wealth. They called in J. C. Hume, veteran Des Moines attorney. Acting under detailed instructions, Hume drew up what is known as the trust indenture of the Hubbell estate. It is said that Hume received a fee of $5,000 for his work, a large amount for the times.

The Hubbell Trust came into being December 31, 1903, or more than 51 years ago. The document was recorded January 22, 1904, in the Polk County Recorder's office. Fred Hubbell then was 63 years old. More than 27 years of his life remained.

Under terms of the document, Hubbell immediately assigned a large portion of his wealth to his estate. He fixed things so that a major part of the estate's assets can not be sold by the heirs until well into the 1980s or 1990s, or perhaps even later.

The trust has stood the tests of time and the courts. The 32-page document has been modified slightly only twice in more than half a century. The legality of the trust has been upheld in test cases.

The indenture contains stern warnings to the Hubbell heirs against becoming "spendthrifts." There was no need, as it happens, for Fred Hubbell to have worried about the caliber of his descendants. The Hubbells of today, in the third and fourth generations, are hard-working, alert and conscientious people.

It appears that the trust is destined to last substantially in its original form for 80 or 90 years. Few human instrumentalities survive so long without major change.

The trust document provides that the estate shall be kept intact until 21 years have elapsed following the death of Beulah C. Wachtmeister and the last of the present trustees. The trustees are Grover C. Hubbell, 72; Frederick W. Hubbell, 63; and James W. Hubbell, 59. The only other trustees the estate ever has had were F. M. himself and Frederick C.

Frederick M. Hubbell had the right under the trust to collect all of the estate's net income each year if he so desired. Actually, the income generally was divided with his children. In the last years of his life, he usually took an annual income of $20,000 for himself.

The present day value of the estate runs well up into the millions. The most valuable item in the assets is stock of the Equitable of Iowa. The estate owns about 80 per cent of that company's stock. The remaining 20 per cent of the outstanding Equitable stock is owned by individual members of the Hubbell family.

Listed in the trust document is all the real estate owned by Hubbell in 1903. That property was divided into two classifications, "A" and "B." Schedule "A" property is not to be sold during the life of the trust. Schedule "B" property may be sold.

There were 108 pieces of Des Moines real estate in the Schedule "A" group originally. A few parcels have been sold for public purposes, such as parks, streets and the like. The trust permits such exceptions. Indeed, the validity of the trust would have been open to question if such sales had not been provided for.

Part of the ground on which the Federal Courthouse stands at East First and Walnut Streets was Schedule "A" Hubbell property at one time. So was part of the ground on which the Des Moines City Hall is located at East First and Grand Avenue.

Most of the property classed as "A" in 1903 still belongs to the estate. One example of this is "Factory

Addition". This large parcel of real estate in general extends from the railroad tracks on the edge of downtown Des Moines south to the Raccoon River and from Twelfth Street on the west to Third Street on the East. Between 70 and 75 per cent of the land in that industrial area belongs to the Hubbell Estate.

Here are some of the addresses of Hubbell Estate properties on Grand, Locust and Walnut Streets in Des Moines:

Grand Avenue—Southeast corner of Second and Grand, 201-05, 207-09, 301-11, 417-19, 509, 607, northwest corner of Eighth and Grand, 809, 900, 1011, 1013, 1101, 1105, 1118, 1207-11, 1212, 1215, 1220-24, northwest corner of Thirteenth and Grand, 1300, 1312, 1327, 1330, 1401-7, 1406, 1409-11, 1413-17, 1418, 1421-24, 1512-16, 1600. East Grand—115, 132, 133, 206, 416, 425, 616, 619, 637, 800, 1500-06, 1654, 1655, 1700-02, 1737-41.

Locust—111, 221, 814-26, 900, 908-10, 920-24, 1100-04, 1101-05, 1119, 1213, 1217-19, 1221, 1321-23, 1402, 1406-10, 1425, 1601. East Locust—400-02, 408, 607-13.

Walnut—906-10, 1021-25, 1022, 1122, 1200, 1326, 1400, 1403-05.

In addition there are properties on West Third Street, West Sixteenth, the Southwest corner of Second and Keo, on High Street, on Tenth, on Cherry, on Keo, on Sixth Avenue, Seventh Street, Twelfth Street, Linden, Mulberry, Tuttle, East Court and elsewhere.

Present income of the estate is divided on the basis of the three children of Mr. and Mrs. Frederick M. Hubbell. Thus, Grover C. Hubbell receives one-third, Countess Beulah Wachtmeister one-third, and Frederick W. and James W. Hubbell divide the other third. (They are the sons of the late Frederick C. Hubbell.)

The trust indenture also provides that the estate shall maintain Terrace Hill during the whole of the trust period. Mr. and Mrs. Grover Hubbell live there now.

The trust document further provides that after the death of Grover "the right to use and occupy said homestead shall vest in . . . Frederick W. Hubbell and James W. Hubbell for their natural lives, in succession, and in the order named . . ." After that, the "oldest lineal male descendant of the trustors" (Mr. and Mrs. F. M. Hubbell) shall have the right to occupy the old home.

In addition to the "not to be sold" properties, the trust listed 59 items which are Class B and which "may be sold," plus 11 contracts of purchase and sale of real estate. Much of this real estate has been sold down through the years.

When the estate finally is liquidated, the property will be distributed among the heirs (of whom there are 44 now) on a "per stirpes" basis. That Latin phrase means one-third each will go respectively to the heirs of Frederick C., of Grover C., and of Countess Wacht-meister.

Frederick W. Hubbell and his brother James W. were small boys when the trust was established. Frederick W. was 12 and James W. 8. Their grandfather expressly provided that both should become trustees when they came of age.

When the trust was created in 1903, Hubbell gave special recognition to his oldest son, Frederick C. The letter still is in the family files. It says in part: "In making final disposition of a portion of my property, it seems to me that I ought to give you some special recognition. You have been associated with me as my partner for almost 17 years. You have been of signal assistance to me in accumulating and caring for my estate during all that time; and because you are the oldest of my children there will necessarily devolve upon you the most of the responsibility during the next few years of managing the trust estate."

The letter says further that Frederick C. had been "a good son, loyal, faithful, sympathetic . . . I have always been happy with you."

The letter informed Frederick C. that his father had assigned to him 832 shares of stock in the Equitable. "I intend to treat all my children from a financial standpoint financially alike," the letter concludes, "but for the reasons above given I want you to have the stock."

The elder Hubbell had no time for anyone who wasted money. Set out in the trust document is a statement giving the trustees power to withhold income from any beneficiaries who "become dissipated, or spendthrifts, bankrupts or insolvent, or unable to pay their just debts."

Also barred from sharing in benefits are any who "pledge, mortgage, encumber, dispose of or anticipate the revenues or income" from the trust. Similarly, the trustees have power to halt a beneficiary's income if a creditor tries to garnish or attach that income in a judicial proceeding. This part of the indenture never has been used.

The document provides that the trustees shall be not less than three nor more than five in number. If the number falls below three for any reason, the remaining trustees may appoint a person to fill the vacancy. If the trustees cannot agree on a selection, the Polk County District Court has the power to fill the vacancy.

At the end of the trust period, the trustees must pay over the "property and estate then remaining" to the "lineal descendants of . . . Frederick C. Hubbell,

Beulah C. Wachtmeister, and Grover C. Hubbell . . ."

In 1907, the Supreme Court of Iowa held the trust valid. In that law suit, the courts estimated that the Hubbell estate would expire in about 1978. It appears now that that estimate was too conservative by a number of years.

In commenting on the estate, the Supreme Court said: "The courts are not interested in building up large estates, but if this should result from the faithful discharge of the obligations of confidence, not inimical to the laws of the land, the administration of the trustees, even though tending to increase the trust estate, ought not to be disapproved."

The opinion said it was Hubbell's privilege to create such a trust if he wanted to. Said the court: "Proverbially, the accumulations of the provident never reach the fourth generation and if in recognition of this, or because of distrust of the business sagacity of those whom he would bestow his bounty (on), the owner elects to tie up his estate during the period of the lives then in being and 21 years thereafter . . . he has the lawful right under the statutes of this state to do so . . ."

Foresighted though he was, Hubbell did not anticipate the rapid growth of Des Moines. The city's population was about 75,000 in 1903. The total now exceeds 180,000.

One "Class A" item in the Hubbell Trust was a farm subsequently bisected by Avenue Frederick M.

Hubbell in northeast Des Moines. The Polk County District Court several months ago allowed the trust to be modified so that that land could be sold. The land consisted of 43.21 acres lying on both sides of Hubbell Avenue and north of Easton Boulevard.

In asking that the trust be changed, the trustees said in their district court petition: "Mr. Hubbell . . . in 1903 . . . had no reason to believe that the City of Des Moines . . . would at this time completely surround the property in question and that its value, if it could be sold for residential purposes, would be nearly 10 times its value as for agricultural land."

The petition placed the 1954 value of the land at $1,500 to $2,000 an acre. The agricultural income, however, was only about $200 in 1954, or less than the real estate taxes levied on the property.

When Frederick M. Hubbell died in 1930, it is said that he left "only his hard derby hat, his gold watch and his goldheaded cane." Everything else had been disposed of. The inventory files in Polk County District Court listed his remaining personal estate at only $1,010. The assets were: Membership in the Des Moines Club (sold after his death) $500; cash in his possession, $10. The watch and the cane, $500.

Everything else except his life insurance had been placed in trust in 1903 and later. He had $18,132.67 in life insurance.

The main structure of the Hubbell Estate has varied little since 1903. Value of the assets, however, is vastly greater. Growth of the Equitable has been fabulous. Also, the value of the real estate has moved upward with the growth of Des Moines and with the expansion of the entire American economy.

Des Moines business leaders generally agree that the trustees have given the Hubbell Estate excellent management and at the same time have followed policies that are fair to those with whom the Hubbells do business.

The estate seems certain to remain impregnable throughout the rest of the trust period, if anything in human life is certain.

What will happen when the time comes to close the estate? Will the property be divided? Or will the assets be placed in a corporation whose earnings will be distributed among the heirs? How many heirs will there be by that time?

The Hubbell Estate was created 10 years before the Federal Government set up its system of taxing personal incomes and corporations. What will the federal taxes be in liquidation?

The answers to these questions are hidden in the distant future.

17

Terrace Hill

TERRACE HILL IS as unlikely as a fairy tale.

By all logic, this magnificent red-brick mansion of Frederick M. Hubbell should have departed long ago. The old home belongs to the age of hoop skirts, of Strauss waltzes, of 19th Century rich who traveled the world and bought art treasures everywhere.

The 20-room home, still occupied by a Hubbell, stands almost alone in its past glory in an 8-acre park of trees on West Grand Avenue in Des Moines. Now 85 years old, the three-story house with the two-story tower is weathered with age.

Time has marched on in the once-fancy residential neighborhood around Terrace Hill. Across the street now is a big new insurance company home office building. Nearby are apartment houses, a bowling alley, a filling station, a "drive-in" restaurant.

Only such a man as Fred Hubbell would have bought Terrace Hill in the first place. Only a man of his temperament and background would have cherished the home so much as to insist on its preservation and occupancy over the span of a century or more.

Only a strong estate would have been capable of bearing the burden of maintaining such a home all these years. The property taxes alone exceed $4,000 a year.

Fred Hubbell loved Terrace Hill as he loved his family. He took care to provide for the old place as if it were another heir. He arranged for the Hubbell Estate to maintain the home throughout the life of the Hubbell Trust.

Mr. and Mrs. Grover Hubbell moved into Terrace Hill in 1924. It is their home now. If they want to, Mr. and Mrs. F. W. Hubbell are next in line to occupy the home. Mr. and Mrs. J. W. Hubbell have the next right. After that, the trust provides, the right to occupy the home shall vest in "the eldest lineal male descendant" of F. M. Hubbell.

Terrace Hill, the trust indenture says, "shall be and remain the homestead of the Hubbell family, and in the possession of the eldest male lineal descendant of the trustors (Mr. and Mrs. F. M. Hubbell), so long as any such descendant lives, during the whole of the trust period aforesaid."

Terrace Hill was built by B. F. Allen, the early Des Moines banker. The work started in 1865 on a site that was then "far out of town." The park on which the home was built then extended from Twenty-second Street to Twenty-eighth Street and from Grand Avenue to the Raccoon River.

Allen had a lot of money and he spared no expense in building his dream mansion. It is said that the structure cost him $250,000, a really amazing amount of money in the post-Civil War period.

Des Moines had no railroad when Terrace Hill was started. Sixteen mule teams hauled the materials across the prairies. In the bumping wagon trains came walnut and rosewood for the high-arched doors and windows, huge quantities of bricks, mahogany for the imposing stairway, large mirrors, six white Italian marble mantels and two pink ones.

The home was completed in time for the Allens' fifteenth wedding anniversary January 29, 1869. Mr. and Mrs. Hubbell were among the guests at the brilliant anniversary party which was one of the most pretentious social events in the history of Des Moines. More than $2,000 was spent for flowers alone. The Allens imported a caterer from Chicago for the affair. That act was a new high for opulence in Des Moines, then a prairie town of 7,000 inhabitants. The banquet spread cost $6,000 and the center bouquet $700.

Fred Hubbell was rising fast in the Des Moines of 1869. Little did he think at the anniversary party, however, that in 15 years this magnificent home would be his—and that Allen would have fallen, crushed by bankruptcy.

Allen came to grief after he went into banking in Chicago. His Chicago operation was unsound to begin with. Then, a depression developed in the 1870s. Allen used up all his Des Moines assets in a vain effort to keep the Chicago bank afloat. He was adjudged bankrupt in 1875.

Hoyt Sherman was named receiver. The law firm of Polk and Hubbell handled the liquidation of Allen's assets. One such asset was Terrace Hill. Allen no longer could afford to live there.

The Allen home was up for sale for perhaps 10 years. The Allens were gone. During that period, a Catholic organization refused to take over Terrace Hill. The Presbyterians talked about acquiring the property for use as a university. (Allen University.) That idea never got beyond the conversation stage.

Hubbell became interested in Terrace Hill. On March 30, 1884, he wrote in his diary: "Went out to see Allen this AM. He wants $55,000 for his homestead."

The diary for May 9, a few weeks later, says: "Accepted Allen's offer for Terrace Hill." On May 11, he wrote: "DeVere (Thompson) and I spent the afternoon at Allen's house." And on May 25, Hubbell proudly reported that he took a Mr. Rockwell "out to see my house."

On August 20, the Hubbells began moving into Terrace Hill. On August 23, Hubbell "went out and slept with Fred (his son) at Terrace Hill." On August 24, "Frances went out to Terrace Hill and slept."

From that day to this, more than 70 years, Terrace Hill has been the Hubbell homestead.

Set 400 feet back from busy Grand Avenue, Terrace Hill seems aloof from mid-20th century life. Out on the street, long lines of moving automobiles are a normal condition. But up the driveway on the wooded hill, it would seem perfectly fitting even now for a carriage drawn by two spanking grays to stop at the front door, and to have two high society ladies of the 1890s step down in their long skirts for an afternoon call.

Historian Cyrenus Cole said Terrace Hill was the "ultra social center of Des Moines" in the Gay Nineties. "A foolish man had built the big place," Cole wrote, "and a wise man was then living in it. The foolish man was a Mr. Allen who wanted to make Des Moines bigger than there was any need of its being . . . In due time, Mr. Hubbell came along and picked up many of the things that Mr. Allen had dropped by the way."

Cole provides this further insight: "Mr. Hubbell was a small man with a low voice. He always smiled and seldom talked, at least out loud. It is said of him that he never lost his head nor his money."

It was in the 1890s, on May 2, 1899, that Terrace Hill was the scene of Des Moines' most brilliant social event of its time—or any time. That was the day when

Beulah Cooper Hubbell, daughter of the rich, self-made Fred Hubbell, married Count Carl Axel Wachtmeister of Sweden.

The event caught the imagination of the whole country. The rich American heiress of the prairies marries European nobility! Grand Avenue was thronged with carriages that chilly spring evening as all Des Moines struggled to catch a glimpse of the couple and the guests. The grounds around Terrace Hill were brightly lighted. Some 700 persons attended the reception.

The most colorful and complete story of that wedding was written by Oliver Newman, then a reporter on the old Des Moines Leader. The Leader was having a quarrel at the time with Hubbell over the waterworks. The Leader, as a consequence, was not invited to cover the wedding.

Newman went anyway. He donned a dress suit, posed as a foreign diplomat and had no trouble at all in crashing the wedding. (There were several legitimate foreign diplomats present.) The Leader next morning carried a 2½-column story under the heading: "Married in Great State."

Throwing all restraint to the winds, Newman wrote:

"Amidst sweet strains of music under the soft lights of a myriad-prism'd chandelier, amidst perfume of flowers and surrounded by distinguished company,

Count Axel Wachtmeister of Sweden and Miss Beulah C. Hubbell were married at Terrace Hill at 7 o'clock last evening.

"It was the most notable social event in Des Moines history uniting the scion of ancient and noble continental line to the daughter of a wealthy American family. The company of guests included representatives of the nobility of European nations, the most select few of Des Moines aristocracy and a noteworthy company from Chicago, Washington and other places where the bride had spent much time.

"It was such a ceremony as well might have been, as it was, the crowning glory of the life of the fair bride. Under the shimmering, many-tinted lights of the great parlor chandelier, with its thousands of cut-glass prisms before an altar of ferns and lillies, with the melodious strains of the Lohengrin wedding march floating softly through the hallways on the perfume-laden air, the happy couple spoke the vows which united ancient title and beauty, wealth and ancestral honor, the off-spring of ancient nobility and the scion of modern progressiveness and enterprise."

Newman apparently was the only reporter present in the wedding parlor, and he took full advantage of the fact that his eye-witness story was exclusive.

"Terrace Hill was never more magnificent than last night," he wrote. "Brightly lighted and embowered with flowers and greenery, it was a very palace.

The great hall seemed almost lonesome while the bridal party was forming for its movement to the parlor in which the wedding was to take place.

"Only 60 or 70 guests were in the house. The bridal party formed at the landing of the great staircase and came down the steps to the strains of the Lohengrin march. The staircase was decorated with smilax, entwined with bunches of white carnations. On the Newell posts were white ribbons and streamers. In the large hall below was an immense bunch of American beauty roses . . .

"Kromer's full orchestra was stationed in the east hall, cut off from the main hall by a bank of palms, and played throughout the evening, save only while the ceremony was in progress."

With a professional eye for detail, Newman reported:

"The ushers, Mr. Harry Prouty and Mr. Raymond Windsor, stood at the foot of the stairway, holding the ribbons that were to form the avenue through which would march the bridal party . . . Mr. DeVere Thompson broke the suspense with the announcement that the party was ready to move. The guests fell back to make room for the formation of the avenue . . . Miss Lucy Runnells, in the parlor door, raised her hand and signalled for the orchestra to start the march, and at the same time the party appeared on the landing . . ."

Newman did not miss any of the color. The story said:

"The bridal party advanced, the Rev. J. Everist Cathell, the celebrant in full vestments, including the red scarf of a doctor of divinity, in the lead . . . The groom was pale but composed. The best man smiled slightly and was perfectly at ease. Next came Miss Mary Wilson of Chicago, the maid of honor and school friend of the bride. She was gowned in cyrano red, cut decollette and sleeveless, carrying pink roses.

"Then came the bride, a picture of composure and looking as happy as a bride should. She wore a white satin brocade court gown in which she was presented at the court of St. James. The skirt and bodice was trimmed in silver, the yoke and sleeves of white illusion.

"The court train was of white brocaded satin, with ruffles of chiffon falling from the shoulders. The train was fully three yards in length and was borne by Frederick W. Hubbell, the little nephew of the bride, clad entirely in white, with white chiffon falling over his wrists."

Frederick W. also wore "white stockings and slippers," the story added, then continued: "The bridal veil was held in place by a tiara of diamonds and pearls, the gift of her parents. On her stock she wore a

coronet of pearls and diamonds, the gift of the groom."
(A stock was a close-fitting wide cravat worn on the
neck.)

Newman reported that Beulah and Carl did not
kiss at the conclusion of the marriage ceremony. The
reporter wrote: "The groom made a movement as if
to kiss the bride but she gently shook her head . . . The
first person to present congratulations was the best man,
followed by a maid of honor who kissed the bride and
shed a tear."

"Mr. and Mrs. Hubbell came next," the story continued. "Mr. Hubbell shook hands with the groom
and kissed his daughter. By this time, Mrs. Hubbell
had passed the groom. She had been greatly affected
throughout the ceremony and had several times turned
her face to the wall and with difficulty suppressed sobs.

"Now she broke down completely, and as she kissed
the bride she drew her face behind her fan, sobbing
convulsively and withdrew, followed by her husband,
himself considerably shaken with emotion."

Newman also described how the presents were displayed "in a room at the north end of the hall on the
second floor."

"The bride's jewels were in a separate cabinet,"
the reporter wrote. "The presents were not nearly so
numerous as at many other Des Moines weddings. The
magnificence of the occasion perturbed the majority of
friends of the family and they were unable to deter-

mine what should be sent to a couple of such high distinction, the result being that fewer presents were sent than might have been expected."

The most munificent of all the presents was not on display. The Iowa State Register that same morning reported: "The most substantial present, it is said, came from her father in the form of a check for $300,000. On this point, however, the family are reticent while not denying the rumor." (Actually, it was the note for $200,000.)

Despite Newman's opinion, the couple seems to have done pretty well in the value and volume of gifts. The groom's parents presented an imposing volume of jewelry and silver receptacles. Oliver H. Perkins sent a set of solid silver service and Gertrude Getchell sent silverplate. DeVere Thompson gave the bride a diamond brooch.

Other gifts included: A dictionary from Miss Mary Rogers of Dubuque; a rocking chair from Mr. and Mrs. Harry West, Fannie West and Charley Chase; a gold pedestal from Robert Cary; a shoe horn of ivory, hand carved with white flowers, from Baron D. Liljencrantz, believed to have been in the Austro-Hungarian consulate in Chicago; a silver soup ladle from Mr. and Mrs. J. H. Windsor and Raymond Windsor; "The River Bend and Other Poems," from the author, Des Moines Poet Tacitus Hussey.

There was a large volume of silver, fans, books and glassware gifts from other friends.

The Leader also said in the wedding story that Beulah was "one of the largest landed property owners in the city." "It has been the policy of Mr. Hubbell to bring up his children to an understanding of the business which must one day come into their hands, of attending to their own property and affairs," the newspaper story said. "To this end, he has settled on his only daughter at various times large amounts of the most valuable property and many leaseholds of great price in the business section of the city and on West Grand Avenue."

Terrace Hill today is not much different than it was on that gala wedding night 56 years ago. The old home, of course, has automatic heat, electric lights and all of the comforts of modern living. Nevertheless, stepping inside the front door gives a visitor the feeling of dropping back into life of the last century.

Des Moines assessors went over Terrace Hill carefully in 1941. In their report, they commented on: "The heavy walnut and rosewood trim on the first and second floors, the ornate mahogany stairway, ornate plaster ceilings, the very high grade interior finish, the elevator, six bathrooms of which one has marble wainscoting and three have tile floors and wainscoting, eight fireplaces, slate roof and exterior walls of solid brick."

The assessors placed a full value of $72,450 on Terrace Hill at that time.

The home, incidentally, did not stand empty after Allen failed. The place was occupied by a caretaker. Terrace Hill was heated in those days by wood-burning stoves. It must have taken a mountain of wood each winter to keep the place warm. There are five big rooms on the first floor, four bedrooms and a sitting room on the second floor, rooms in the basement and on the third floor.

Fred Hubbell left his mark on Terrace Hill in many ways. Most spectacular is the big stained glass window at the head of the stairway, installed sometime after 1884. (Edna Ferber once called that stairway "a continuous mahogany ribbon running from floor to floor.") Hubbell also converted the third floor from a ballroom into suites for servants.

Terrace Hill originally had a roof reservoir that gathered rain water for use in the house. Hubbell replaced that system with modern plumbing. He bought the fabulous rock-crystal chandelier in the drawing room. He installed a central heating plant in the stable to replace the old stoves.

At the time of Beulah's wedding, a staff of 12 servants was needed to keep Terrace Hill functioning. (It takes five or more now.)

In 1924, when Fred Hubbell was 85 years old, Terrace Hill went through major remodeling. The bill came to more than $50,000. An elevator was installed to enable the aging capitalist to get around his house. Sags in the staircase and elsewhere were corrected. The heating plant was moved into the basement. The house was completely electrified. Clearing out the gas pipes so that electric wires could be installed was an almost endless job.

Grover spearheaded the drive to rejuvenate the old home in 1924. His father was dubious. On June 25, 1924, the elder Hubbell wrote: "A lot of men here tearing the house to pieces according to Grover's wishes. I don't like it. They claim to be improving it." On July 31, Hubbell wrote sadly: "No chance for hot water, so I shaved with cold water."

Careful person that he was, Fred Hubbell decided in 1900 that he ought to have an inventory of the contents of Terrace Hill. He listed everything in the house, down to the last paperweight (value $1).

The 1900 list of 592 items is fascinating to an antique hunter (or a lover of art objects). Most of the items are still in the house. Here were a few listed in 1900, and the rooms in which they were located:

Vestibule—One wrought iron lantern, one Smyrna rug, one brass ornament three feet high.

Lower hall—Two oak carved chairs, one carved rosewood table, one Chinese embroidered center-piece, one Dresden vase, one Turkish silk gold-embroidered banner, six feet by 13 feet, one inlaid table, one Japanese bronze jardinier, one steel engraving of Washington Irving, one large Chinese bronze vase, one ebony stand (elephant), portraits of Isaac Cooper and his wife.

Library—One mahogany secretary, one Chinese lacquer plaque, one bronze Chinese group, a cherry rocker, one tall bronze vase with dragons, one Japanese bell, one old Dresden vase, one mahogany pedestal, one onyx-base lamp, one birch rocker with cushions, one Chinese cloisonne vase, one Chinese figure on red lacquer standard, one Sevres bowl, one enameled tea strainer, one piece Venetian glass two feet high, one picture F. M. Hubbell, one pitcher Hungarian ware, one round cherry table, one red and blue vase, 30 inches high.

Parlor—One Satsuma vase 27 inches high, one statuary marble mantel and pier glass 5½ feet by 8 feet, one cut-glass vase hobnail, one miniature of Beulah, one ornamental thermometer, one large French bowl with red flowers and bird decoration, one pair of Japanese cloisonne vases, one Chinese vase chocolate and blue, one German drinking mug, one very old Saxe vase, one Venetian glass lamp, one portrait in oil of Beulah.

Music room—One mahogany chair with velour upholstery, two small Persian rugs, one Angora goat rug, one onyx ostrich egg.

Drawing room—One statuary marble mantel, one rosewood mantel glass 5½ feet by 8 feet, one rosewood pier glass 5½ feet by 11 feet.

West room—One Romeo and Juliet on marble pedestal, one oil painting, "The Last Days of the Venetian Republic," one cabinet, one glass ornament.

Dining room—One Champlain marble fireplace with oak mantel glass, brass fire set, fender and wood receiver, one red and gold Venetian glass punch bowl.

Frequently there are many units of one item. For example, 48 blue and gold dinner plates with platters to match are listed as just one item. The many laces and embroideries included a costly India shawl, Swiss embroidered handkerchiefs, 11 Irish linen table cloths, an embroidered piano cover, and so on.

Mrs. F. M. Hubbell bought many of these art objects in her 19th century travels in this country and around the world. She bought more after 1900. Grover has added to the treasure also. Thus, Terrace Hill today is even more of an art museum than it was half a century ago. Many items are locked in the built-in vault in the cellar.

Also, to this day, a few pieces of furniture that date back to the Allen era are in use in the Hubbell home. One such item is an old love seat.

What is to become of Terrace Hill? Homes, like humans, have a life to live. They are young, reach adulthood, become middle-aged, grow old and die.

That happens, even in cases where a building somehow stays sound as the passing decades pile up. Each generation has its own way of living. The mansion of 1869 does not fit the specifications of the dream home of 1955.

It is said that the late Frederick C. Hubbell did not choose to move into Terrace Hill during his lifetime. Perhaps the Hubbells of the future will prefer to live elsewhere.

The ultimate fate of Terrace Hill is one of the many fascinating Hubbell mysteries that only time will solve.

18

Poker

FRED HUBBELL ACCUMULATED millions of dollars from business transactions between 1894 and 1922.

His diary shows that in the same 28-year period, he also had a net loss of $184.10 from poker.

He liked to play poker for modest stakes. (Probably a 25-cent limit.) He and his cronies had a club they called the Owls. They usually met at each other's houses on Saturday nights. Hubbell recorded the outcome of many such games in his diary. On January 25, 1910, he wrote: "Went to (H. C.) Alverson's for Owl Club. And took home for my time $28.50."

That probably was the best poker night of his life. In no other game recorded in the diary were his winnings that high. Indeed, he lost oftener than he won. On June 5, 1914, he reported: "1908 to June 4, 1914—175 nights at $1.21 per night, or $211.85 lost."

The diary reports not only his own gains and losses but those of other players as well. On June 19, 1903, for example: "Had Owls at my house tonight. Results. HAE plus $3, CWG plus $6, PJM plus $7.10, Minus FMH $9, Fullerton $5, JHW $2.10. Ed Chase even."

The other players included H. A. Elliott, C. W. Gilmore, Pleasant J. Mills, Robert Fullerton, J. H. Windsor and Ed Chase.

The Owls at various times also included the following: Albert B. Cummins, Iowa's onetime great senator and governor, C. C. Prouty, J. W. Howell, W. R. Warfield, W. O. and E. C. Finkbine, Henry Grefe, Alverson, Charles Hewitt, George Van Evera and other individuals prominent in Des Moines' earlier days.

Hubbell did little gambling when he was young. Money was too important to him. It hurt to lose, as this January 30, 1857, diary entry at Sioux City shows: "Played billiards with Chamberlain and got beat which will end my gambling for the present."

The diary shows that he played a little euchre in the 1880s. But there is no mention of stakes.

The first time the word "poker" appears in the diary is May 5, 1894. Hubbell was a nationally known capitalist by that time. He must have been exposed to poker before that date. Or else he caught on to the game in a hurry.

There was a party of some sort at the Hubbell home that day. The men started a poker game. To his delight, Hubbell won $10.75. He was the big winner. Windsor got clipped for $10.80 and Cummins lost $5.60. Cummins was $5.60 in debt to Hubbell when the game broke up.

There was another game the next night. This time Hubbell won $9.95. Cummins was the big loser with a deficit of $8.15. Windsor dropped $6.25 in the second game.

Cummins didn't play often, and he rarely won. He had two bad sessions in 1903. (He was governor of Iowa then.) On August 22 that year he dropped $20.50. And on November 14 he lost another $20. What would Cummins' church-going followers have thought had they known he played a little poker? Some of them wouldn't have liked it, probably.

Hubbell played little poker after World War I. He was getting to be an old man by that time. Apparently his last game was January 17, 1922, at his 83rd birthday party at Terrace Hill. The guest of honor did not do well. Hubbell lost $4.85. A bigger loser, however, was Federal Judge Martin Wade. He dropped $7.10.

Poker was only a small part of Fred Hubbell's social life. He was fond of big parties. He put on as many at Terrace Hill as his wife's health and his own business activities would allow.

He never let an anniversary or a birthday slip by without a party if he could help it. For example, on

May 7, 1905, exactly half a century ago today, his diary says: "Gave a party in honor of my 50th anniversary of arrival in Des Moines, May 7, 1855. There were present: P. M. Casady, Simon Casady, George M. Hippee, George B. Hippee, J. H. Windsor, L. H. Bush, L. Harbach, E. R. Clapp, Chas. W. Rogg, H. C. Potter, F. C. Hubbell, F. M. Hubbell."

Ten years prior to that date also was a big occasion. On May 7, 1895, he wrote: "Forty years ago today I arrived here in Des Moines. Wishing to remember the day, I invited to dinner P. M. Casady, Hoyt Sherman, George G. Wright, H. C. Potter, E. R. Clapp, J. C. Savery, J. S. Polk, G. M. Hippee, Jas. Callanan, J. A. T. Hull, J. B. Stewart. Dinner at 7. Dispersed at 10 p.m. Good time they said. Wanted me to send for them again at the end of another forty years."

He kept careful track of his social obligations. At the end of the 1918 diary he lists friends to whom "I am indebted to dinner." The list included Clyde L. Herring, J. L. Parrish, Fred Sargent, E. T. Meredith.

Hubbell attended all kinds of functions, in Des Moines and elsewhere. He liked the theater. An 1881 entry, written in New York, says: "Daly's Theater tonight. Needles and Pins" (which was the current hit.) On October 20, 1882, he told of seeing "Mary Anderson in Pigmaleon." He attended a play practically every time he went to New York.

ALBERT B. CUMMINS   CHARLES S. DENMAN

CHESTER C. COLE   B. F. KAUFFMAN, SR.

JAMES H. WINDSOR

G. M. HIPPEE

JAMES CALLANAN

JAMES S. CLARKSON

There is a touch of mirth in a February 7, 1883, entry which says: "Temperance convention today. Big time."

He went to horse races and amusement parks on occasion. August 2, 1889, he wrote: "Saratoga. I took Beulah to the races. The track was all mud and it rained hard. We saw four races and then came home."

Note that he said nothing about betting on the horses. Undoubtedly he closely examined the practice of wagering on horses — and kept his money in his pocket. He sometimes went to Coney Island while he was in New York. But the diary carried no report on what he saw there.

In the 1890s he for some reason mentioned having "wine and cigars" at dinners he gave at Terrace Hill. On April 21, 1895, he wrote: "Gave a dinner today at my house with wine, cigars, etc., to Judge Kinney, C. H. Robinson, Samuel Strauss, Allten Dawson and E. H. Hunter."

He frequently traveled around Iowa for special gatherings. On June 18, 1910, he was in Dubuque for the "Colonial Wars Society. Banquet at Wales house."

In 1906, Hubbell joined a party of Iowans who went into the southern states to visit (and help dedicate in some instances) memorials to the state's Civil War soldiers. There is a feeling of solemnity in this simple language of the diary for November 17, 1906: "Woke up at Andersonville—walked to the cemetery where 13,900 prisoners sleep. Governor Cummins made a very beautiful speech receiving the monument from Capt. Brewer. Mrs. Cummins unveiled the monument and Gen. Carmer accepted in a fine tribute to the dead soldiers in behalf of the U.S."

Andersonville, in Georgia, was the location of a notorious Confederate prison camp.

On November 23, 1906, the Iowa visitors stopped at Pittsburg Landing in Tennessee, the site of a Civil War battle in which Iowa regiments distinguished themselves. "At Pittsburg Landing," the diary says. "Beautiful day. Walked with Godfrey and DeVere to the camp grounds of the 2nd Iowa. Saw Gen. Tuttle monument. Campfire in the evening at which many spoke and told stories."

Forty years ago, people used to celebrate the birthdays of military heroes much more than they do now. On April 27, 1914, Hubbell wrote: "Gen. Grant's birthday celebrated at Grant Club, Des Moines. Dinner at 6:30. Cresswell McLaughlin made a mighty poor address."

Hubbell went to Europe a couple of times in his life and around the world at least once. In 1892, he and Oliver H. Perkins made the world trip. They went by rail to the west coast and took a ship to Australia. The diary is particularly fragmentary in this period, partly because of seasickness. For three consecutive days, the diary says only: "Sick today." On the fourth: "Convalescent again. Life is now worth living."

In the Hawaiian Islands, Hubbell and Perkins went on horseback to see a volcano. Hubbell wasn't so much impressed by the cone as he was by this fact: "Women rode astride."

For days at a time while at sea, the daily entry was limited to one word: "Water." At Samoa he "called on the king. Sat on a mat and drank coconut milk to which his servants treated us. Sailed at 3 p.m. Samoans are a fine race of people."

Still suffering from seasickness, he wrote May 23: "It still storms and I continue melancholy tho I have introduced my stomach to a bottle of champagne which stayed where I put it. More than I can say for anything else on this ship."

In Australia, he became surfeited with sightseeing at one point. On June 11, he wrote: "I walked down the cliff about 300 feet and when I got back I told Oliver I was so full of scenery that I could not hold any more today."

They evidently did not enjoy themselves in that southern-hemisphere. On June 5, Hubbell wrote that "we almost froze." "Oliver complains of the cold a good deal," he said. "We are globe-trotting, and having fun, however."

Hubbell tried to mix in a little business with his overseas pleasure travels. When in London on the world trip, he called on bankers to try to recruit them to sell American railroad bonds. The English apparently were not interested. Here is a sample diary entry (August 4, 1892) : "In London—Went downtown and ordered some clothes. Visited the Bank of England. Got our mail at the Alliance Bank. Visited the Tower of London. Saw the Crown Jewels. Crown worth a billion dollars. Went down to my tailors. Saw Wellington's tomb and St. Paul's. Went to St. George's Club in the evening to meet Mr. Holdtharm who reported he could not sell bonds." (He didn't explain why he thought the crown was worth a billion.)

Hubbell and Perkins sailed from Liverpool, September 6. "Went aboard the Bothnia at 4 p.m.," Hubbell wrote. "She is old, slow and the cellar in which our berths are is moldy and does not smell right, but one can't expect everything for $75."

Hubbell was a railroad man and as such he didn't think he should have to pay railroad fare anywhere in the world. He was just another passenger in Australia, however. On June 6, 1892, he went to see the Australian secretary of railroads, seeking passes from Sydney to Brisbane.

The secretary did not give them passes. Instead, he "referred us to the American consul." Hubbell knew he wouldn't get passes from the consul. Fred thereupon wrote resignedly: "I think we will pay our fare to Brisbane." He wrote no more about that incident. Evidently he and Oliver did pay their fares.

19

Color

"KELLY'S ARMY OF tramps passed our house today."

Fred Hubbell wrote that lone sentence in his diary for April 29, 1894. That was all he said about a famous event in Des Moines history.

"General" Charles Kelly led about 1,000 unemployed men on a march from the west to Washington, D.C. They wanted help from congress. The country was in the grip of the depression of the 1890s, one of the worst economic downturns the United States ever has experienced. Jack London, the noted author, was among the marchers.

Kelly's Army was around Des Moines for a couple of days. The men caused no trouble. They built some rafts out of lumber donated by Des Moines citizens. The Army finally floated out of town down the Des Moines river.

Hubbell was a wealthy man in 1894. Terrace Hill was (and is) a beautiful mansion. What a subject for a painting is suggested by the diary entry—Kelly's ragtag army marching down Grand avenue past Terrace Hill!

In hundreds of ways Hubbell's terse diary gives little glimpses into the color of his life and his times. On November 17, 1856, he wrote in Sioux City: "Bought some whisky to put prickly ash bark into." Prickly ash is a kind of a shrub. Evidently the pioneers mixed prickly ash bark with whisky for medicinal purposes.

Hubbell frequently commented on the medical practices of early Iowa. He often had a sore throat. He visited Dr. Hunt in Sioux City for treatment. On September 18, 1857, Hubbell wrote: "I do not think that Hunt's caustic which he uses so freely in my throat is doing one particle of good. On the contrary, it is doing harm."

On April 1, 1858, the doctors evidently decided the throat needed drastic treatment. The diary says: "Had my palate cut off today and found it was quite painful. Came home and went to bed and slept most of the afternoon."

Hubbell sometimes "treated" his ailments himself. On April 18, 1857, he reported: "Felt a little unwell and took some rhubarb this forenoon." (Rhubarb was a food for ailing stomachs in those days.)

Frontier dentistry also is touched on occasionally in the diary. He had three teeth filled in Des Moines in 1857. On January 4, 1858, he wrote: "Doct Sanborn was over and bored a hole in one of my front teeth that I had filled in Des Moines last winter." The diary doesn't say why the hole was bored, or what good that did.

The American dollar was an entirely different proposition in 1855 than it is in 1955. Hubbell reported on May 16, 1855: "Very pleasant day. Wrote all day. Purchased a hat, coat and a pair of shoes last evening and gave four dollars for them."

A "milliner" evidently was more than a hatter for milady in early Iowa. Hubbell wrote April 16, 1857: "Went down and drew Father's money and went to the milliner and paid them $4.50 for Solon's shirts."

Also, a shirt did not wear out all at once then, as it does now. On September 18, 1858, Hubbell wrote: "Took my shirts down to Putnam's to be mended and new bosoms put in."

Postoffices were different places in the 1850s than they are now. On February 25, 1856, Hubbell went to the postoffice and "bought wax and sand." Wax was commonly used to seal letters. Sand was used instead of a blotter.

As previously mentioned, sleeping frequently was a problem on the frontier. Hubbell had a crisis on that point April 1, 1857. "Weare came after the bedstead," he wrote in Sioux City. "I slept on the floor." Evidently the bed Hubbell had been using belonged to Mr. Weare.

Winter travel was particularly hazardous a century ago. On December 13, 1856, en route from Sioux City to Des Moines, Hubbell's party got lost in a snowstorm near the town of Ashton in Monona county.

"Got lost, turned around, bounced the horses and Providence directed us into Ashton again," he wrote. In later reminiscences, he said: "Left Ashton on the way to Des Moines. We got out about four miles when it began to snow so hard and the snow was so deep we could not proceed any further; so we unhitched the horses from the sleds and each got a horse or a mule and started back to Ashton in the most dreadful snowstorm I had ever seen. We were lucky to get back to town. If we had missed it, we would have frozen to death."

The party "did not attempt to go on," he continued. "In fact, did not want to go. Nothing to read. Very dull. Slept upon the floor in the bar room. Do not expect to get off for a week."

There were no automobiles to crack up in those days. Nevertheless, traffic accidents did take place in Des Moines. On January 2, 1857, he wrote: "Miss Reese, a relative of Hoyt Sherman, was seriously last evening injured by the turning over in a sleigh."

Hubbell frequently was worried in his younger days about social propriety. On September 17, 1857, he wrote: "Feel pretty well and try to be serious. I believe I have not used profane language today."

He wondered whether dancing was an acceptable activity. "Talked with Col. Wood about dancing,"

Hubbell reported January 31, 1857. "He thinks it is all right." Hubbell then talked to the dancing master. The terms were "$6 for four lessons. I should like to go very much." He did, on February 11.

"Major and myself took a lesson in dancing this forenoon at 11 o'clock," he wrote. "Commenced with the polka." After that, he went to dances frequently. He was shocked at a dance February 22, 1858, in Sioux City. The women were drinking. "Went over to the Pacific House to see the party at the ball," he wrote. "There were a great many Dutch and French population and they were drinking wine, ladies and all. Concluded it was too deep for me."

This was an age when a fellow sparked a girl by playing cards with her. On June 2, 1858, Hubbell "got acquainted with Miss Griffey. We played muggins some." On June 8, he "was over to see Miss Jamison this evening. Played muggins and euchre." "Muggins" is either a card game, or a domino contest. Euchre is a card game.

Swimming in the Floyd river at Sioux City was quite a summertime sport in those days. Hubbell loved the water. So did a lot of others. On July 18, 1857, he wrote: "Went up the Floyd to take a swim but could not get a good place." Swimming was in the nude. The self-conscious pioneers probably scattered widely along the river bank. That may have been the reason why Hubbell "could not get a good place."

You may think that gymnasium equipment is a modern development. Not so. The health-conscious Hubbell wrote May 26, 1858: "Plumb put up the vaulting bar today and it is very fine." The next day Hubbell went back and "exercised on the vaulting bar some."

Hubbell was a capitalist of some national repute when he resumed keeping a daily diary in the 1880s. He made numerous trips to New York, Chicago, Philadelphia, St. Louis and elsewhere for business reasons.

Usually, the diary entries are devoted exclusively to business matters on those trips. But he did give a little insight into what a topflight 19th century businessman did with his spare time while away from home.

On May 24, 1883, he was in Washington and he "called on Washington monument. Liked it. Also visited capitol and paid 50c to young man to show me through." The next day he took in "Corcoran's art gallery. Rebecca at the Well best thing I saw."

He appeared to have been a little lonely away from home at times. On Sunday, December 13, 1896, he was in Boston. "Slept til noon," he wrote. "Took lunch at 1 p. m. Read newspaper til 4. Rode on streetcar til dark and then to bed."

Those who believe that the "key clubs" of today are a relatively modern invention will be surprised by Hubbell's February 8, 1898, report written in Portland, Maine. "Bird took me to his club at Cumberland and gave me a drink of whiskey out of his own decanter," the diary says. "No bar. Every member keeps his own jug under lock and key."

Hubbell sometimes saw famous political figures on his eastern trips. On January 23, 1892, he called on Senator William Allison of Iowa in Washington and "talked silver with him." That is the only reference in the Hubbell diary to the famous national political battles of the late 19th and early 20th century over whether unlimited amounts of silver could be coined into money.

In 1894, Hubbell went to Washington to try to procure the appointment of Des Moines postmaster for E. H. Hunter. The postmaster general gave "no encouragement." "Then to the White House," the diary says. "Waited a long time. Finally Mr. Thurber, private secy to (President) Grover Cleveland, said we would prejudice our case if we went in (to see the president), so we concluded not to." Hunter got the postal appointment anyway.

Hubbell briefly mentions some notable current events in his diary, and omits others. On June 6, 1884, he wrote: "Blaine nominated today. Fred wrote from Paris . . ."

That's all the space the Republican nominee for president rated in the diary. The fact that Hubbell was a Democrat does not explain the brief mention. Cleveland, who was the Democratic nominee for president that year (and winner in the general election), wasn't even mentioned in the diary in that year.

On April 30, 1889, Hubbell wrote: "A hundred years ago today Washington was inaugurated as president. The boys are celebrating." Would Americans of today celebrate the 100th anniversary of a famous president? Perhaps not. There will be such an opportunity in 1961, when the centennial of Abraham Lincoln's first inauguration as president will be observed.

Hubbell nearly always was on hand when a famous person visited Des Moines. On March 1, 1912, he wrote: "Went to the Coliseum and listened to Woodrow Wilson speak on Back to the People."

The next day Hubbell "called at the Savery and was introduced to Woodrow Wilson and took him with John Cownie and Mr. Magill to Highland Park College. Mr. Wilson made an address there. Then I took him to the capitol to call on Gov. Carroll, then to the Savery where I left him . . ." Wilson was elected president that fall.

On February 12, 1914, Hubbell "went up to University Place Church to see Helen Keller, deaf, dumb and blind girl." On October 29, that same year: "W. J. Bryan at the Coliseum tonight. I went and heard a good speech." On September 6, 1919, Hubbell "went to the Coliseum this evening. 10,000 or more were there to hear President Wilson speak about the treaty of peace and the League of Nations. "I had a seat on the platform."

On April 14, 1916, Hubbell regretfully had to pass up an opportunity to eat dinner with the original Henry Ford at Clyde L. Herring's house. But Hubbell did get to lunch with Ford. The diary says: "Clyde Herring invited me to lunch at Des Moines Club to hear Henry Ford who makes Ford cars. I sat next to him. Good time. I was invited to dinner at Mr. Herring's house but could not go because I feared the sheriff would service notice of appeal on the 5th st. case and call me out from dinner to serve me. The sheriff came to my house three times between 6:30 and 11 p.m. to serve me."

In his later years, Hubbell continually urged that the nations of the world take steps to prevent future wars. As long ago as 1914, right before the outbreak of World War I, he said: "I would like to see war abandoned. What could be more foolish than for nations to keep on building those dreadnaughts that cost ten millions apiece and ten millions more to run and then go on the junk pile in about ten years?

"I had a plan to get England, France, Japan and the United States to go together and agree to stand by each other in case of aggression from any outside power. But one of our senators (probably Cummins) assures me that congress would never enact legislation looking to sending American men or American money into defense of a European nation."

How wrong that senator was! Less than four years later, Hubbell's two grandsons were in the American army which fought World War I to save the Allies of Europe. And still another generation later, Hubbell's great grandsons were in service in a Second World War fought in part to save again those same Allies.

The 1914 Hubbell statement continues: "Now I favor a trust in battleships. I would have these four nations maintain their present equipment and agree to lend their battleships to the nations attacked. With such an agreement, none of the nations mentioned would need to build any more warships. I favor any plan that will cut down the enormous cost of war and the preparation for war."

In that same statement, Hubbell took a strong stand for women's rights. "I hope to live long enough to see women given every right men have," he said. "Men know that women are better. They are educated. They own property. Why should they not have equal rights? I want to see women vote because they will vote to improve many things that ought to be improved. I do not want to pose as a prohibitionist but the saloon will be abolished some day and the women vote will do it."

Permanent peace did not come in Hubbell's time, of course. National prohibition went into effect in 1920, but was repealed in 1933 after his death. (He died in 1930.) Women got the unrestricted right to vote in 1920.

20

Master of All Trades

"SPECIALIZE IN A particular field of business or in a profession," young men of today are told. "Don't be a jack of all trades and a master of none."

Fred Hubbell's career is an example of how wrong textbooks can be in individual cases. Rarely has any man been so successful in so many fields. As has been pointed out before, Hubbell was a notable railroad builder and operator, a waterworks executive, an insurance company founder and president, a tremendous real estate investor, a capable attorney.

Any one of these attainments would have been achievement enough for the average man. But the Hubbell list doesn't stop there. He also was in on: Mutual telephone companies, coal mines, the Des Moines packing plant, insurance companies other than the Equitable, a number of Des Moines banks.

In addition, he invested in a gold mine investment in California (the record doesn't show how well he fared on this flyer). And he lent small sums of money to persons in modest circumstances and large sums to well-known Iowans. He even went to Ottumwa one time to investigate the possibilities of establishing a strawmill there. (That idea apparently did not work out.)

Nevertheless, it isn't quite true to say that Hubbell was not a specialist. He was a specialist, in fact a genius, in the field of making money.

He had considerable help in his enterprises, of course. His sons and grandsons were his active lieutenants, as were DeVere Thompson, August Denman, Jacob Wagner and Chris Huttenlocher. Thompson was active in real estate and railroading. Denman was in charge of the waterworks. Wagner was superintendent of the Des Moines Union. Huttenlocher long was an important administrative official in the Hubbell office. But Hubbell himself was the kingpin in the complex empire that he founded.

His practice of never passing up an opportunity to make money sometimes took him and his associates down strange paths. In the 1880s, the bonds and warrants of counties and cities in Iowa, Kansas, Nebraska and elsewhere in the middlewest were not worth much at times. That paper often could be bought for 25 to 50 cents on the dollar.

Hubbell felt certain these obligations would rise in value and probably would be worth full par value some day. He had had considerable experience in such transactions at Sioux City in his early days in Iowa. He supplied DeVere Thompson and his son, Fred C.

Hubbell, with a quantity of gold coins. He sent them out to buy up all the bonds and warrants that were available at a sizable discount.

Thompson later told how he wrapped himself in a buffalo robe and journeyed by sleigh through several states in the wintertime buying up warrants. "The setup was so lucrative for Hubbell that Thompson complained," one Hubbell employee recalled. "Thompson wanted a share of the profits. Hubbell took him in on the deal."

A few hints of this program survive in the diaries. On Oct. 1, 1885, for example, Hubbell reported: "DeVere started for Kansas." (A warrant-buying trip, probably.) On January 20, 1886, he reminded himself: "Write Nance County, Nebraska." He probably had some of that county's warrants in his possession. A January 2, 1887 entry says: "Write Ford County treasurer about redemptions." There is a Ford county in Kansas.

After buying warrants, Thompson and young Hubbell frequently sought to convince the counties and cities that such paper should be made a general obligation of the local government. If that could be arranged, the value of the paper would be increasd.

Such a change, however, necessitated local elections on that point. Local officials and taxpayers frequently were opposed to the idea. Thompson and young Fred more than once found themselves in difficulties. There is a story in the Hubbell family of an irate Kansas crowd which threatened to hang young Hubbell. Due to his youth, they let him go.

Both Thompson and F. C. Hubbell became partners in F. M. Hubbell, Son & Company at the time of the organization of that company in 1887. The firm is one of the major property owners in Des Moines today. Among other things, the company owns the west half of the main Younker store building, and, together with Trustees of the Hubbell Estate, the ground on which the Insurance Exchange Building is located at Fifth and Grand.

The Hubbell Estate now owns one-third of F. M. Hubbell, Son & Company, Incorporated. One-third belongs to other heirs and the final third to The Thompson Trust, which was established many years ago by DeVere Thompson.

The diary and papers say little about Hubbell's purchases of Des Moines real estate. Yet, the present Hubbell properties in Des Moines are valued at many millions of dollars.

The lack of references to property in the diary is understandable. The diary was not meant to be a complete record of Hubbell's life and dealings. Rather, the diary primarily served as a personal reminder in matters of pending importance.

No person believed more profoundly in real estate for investment purposes than did Hubbell. He owned real estate as a 16-year-old boy in Des Moines and as a 17- and 18-year-old in Sioux City. He bought property again after he returned to Des Moines in 1861. A 1925 newspaper story says: "The railroad reached Iowa City in 1855. It did not get to Des Moines until more than 10 years after that. Mr. Hubbell came just ahead of the break and got his foothold and stayed. He believed in Des Moines real estate and bought and held. He engaged in many enterprises but he never lost sight of downtown Des Moines real estate."

Hubbell himself said in an interview in the 1920s that he had bought Des Moines property as long as 60 years before. He denied in that interview that he was worth 25 million dollars but he said: "I don't know exactly what I'm worth. When I buy a piece of property I put it on the books at cost price. I don't try to pad its value by gradually multiplying it on the books . . ."

In the same interview, he described this technique for becoming wealthy: "I would buy a piece of land. Then I would pay for it. Then I would rent it to someone, collect the rent. With the money gathered as rent, when it amounted to enough, I would buy another piece of land, pay for it, rent it, and continue the process indefinitely."

In a 1925 talk to Des Moines real estate men, Hubbell said: "I never speculate. You have to speculate in Florida; to buy and hope for the best. If you buy in Des Moines, you are certain what you buy will be worth more in 5 or 10 years."

The Hubbell diaries provide revealing glimpses into the troubles of newspapers in Des Moines in the late 19th century. The diaries disclose the fact that the Des Moines Leader was in precarious condition in the 1880s and that J. S. "Ret" Clarkson, editor of The Iowa State Register, had his financial difficulties also.

The Leader probably was in trouble because of the intense competition in the newspaper field. (In 1886, Des Moines had five daily newspapers.) On the other hand, Clarkson could have become involved because of his outside interests. He was forever delving into such nonjournalistic enterprises as railroad building. In addition, he was a nationally important Republican politician. He was chairman of the national Republican executive committee in the early 1890s and was first assistant postmaster general in that same period.

The Register and the Leader were competitors in the morning newspaper field. Even so, Clarkson wanted Hubbell to put up $7,500 to buy the Leader's way into the Northwestern Associated Press. Clarkson may have been trying to protect his own secret and indirect interest in the Leader. The Hubbell diary in 1881 said the Leader owed Clarkson $900.

With his usual thoroughness, Hubbell investigated the condition of the Leader. He found that paper had only 1,100 daily subscribers in August of 1881. That was a very small circulation, even for those times.

On June 8, 1883, Lowry W. Goode, editor of the Leader, came to see Hubbell. Goode, the diary says, "told me he would have to fail up and wanted me to hunt up a customer for the Leader." Hubbell talked to Ret and his brother Dick Clarkson about buying the Leader. Hubbell was personally interested because by that time he had endorsed a $2,500 note of L. W. and F. D. Goode.

Ret, however, was in no position to buy the Leader. Ret himself owed Hubbell $17,122 at the time. This debt may have stemmed from railroad dealings in which both Clarkson and Hubbell participated. Clarkson went even further in debt the next year. The diary says Clarkson owed $25,000 on February 3, 1884.

Clarkson survived his financial crisis and so did the Leader. It is not possible to tell from the diary whether Hubbell had anything to do with their recovery.

The Leader's return to solvency apparently was not a permanent improvement. In 1896 the paper was in trouble again. Hubbell went to Chicago to see Roswell Miller, president of the Milwaukee Railroad, about getting some help for the Leader. The diary shows that the railroad was willing to help the Leader, for a price.

Here is what the diary said Miller wanted from the newspaper: "First, refrain from supporting measures detrimental to the interests of railroads. Second, without being aggressive or controversial, the tone of his newspaper should be such as to discourage the passing of measures detrimental to the roads. Third: Should expect his paper to make such tempered comment on pending detrimental measures in such tone as would influence a legislature and public against them and against such measures becoming law. Fourth: The comments to be in a persuasive and conciliatory vein, indicating that the editor was of the opinion the proposed measures were not needed for the public welfare."

The railroads were ruthless rulers of the midwest. in those days. They were powerful in Washington as well. They were the political and economic giants of their time. Many newspapers did their bidding.

There is no evidence to indicate, however, that the Leader subjected itself to any such terms as those proposed by Miller.

Hubbell was curious about the final outcome of the Leader's bid to the Milwaukee. On April 19, 1896, he wrote a note in his diary to remind him to ask Miller about it the next time he saw him. On October 21, the same year, the diary quotes Miller as saying, "They (the Milwaukee) did nothing for the press last winter." Miller evidently didn't feel that he had to spend much in that field. Miller said a G. B. Pray (apparently a public relations man) "managed things and had but little money."

The Leader had a rough time of it throughout the 1890s and The Iowa State Register wasn't riding high either. (A January 10, 1897 diary entry reminded Hubbell to see Clarkson about a $3,000 debt dating back to February 28, 1895.) The Register and the Leader were consolidated in 1902. In 1903, Gardner Cowles and Harvey Ingham bought the paper and started The Register and Tribune on their way to becoming the strong publications that they are today.

Financing newspaper editors constituted a small part of Hubbell's private loans. He lent money to some of the big Iowa names of his era, such as Charles E. Rawson, later United States senator; Railroad Man John Runnells, and A. B. Cummins, famed attorney who became governor and United States senator.

Hubbell signed notes for $50,000 December 31, 1907, for Rawson at the old Iowa National Bank. The notes enabled Rawson to get securities from the bank with which to pay up his stock in the old Des Moines Life Insurance Company. "They gave me $5,000 for my name," Hubbell reported. Rawson also posted as security $50,100 of his life insurance stock, plus various items of real estate and a $54,000 life, accident and fire insurance policy.

Hubbell frequently provided financing for Cummins, his friend and his attorney. As early as 1893,

Hubbell endorsed notes totaling $5,500 for Cummins at the Des Moines Savings Bank. And in 1903, Cummins, then governor of Iowa, paid Hubbell $29,880, apparently in settlement of debts.

For all his dealings with Cummins, Hubbell appears never to have tried to influence the attorney in matters of railroad policy, or in politics.

Cummins often was Hubbell's attorney in railroad negotiations. Yet, Cummins was a Progressive Republican and a mortal foe of the railroads in late 19th century and early 20th century Iowa politics.

Cummins was elected governor in 1902, 1904 and 1906. Every time the railroads fought him. In the end, Cummins won a complete victory. He seized control of the Republican state conventions from the railroads. More important, he pushed through the legislature bills that drastically curbed railroad power.

One of Cummins' measures forbade railroads issuing free passes to anyone. Up to that time, the railroads gave passes to members of the legislature, state officials and other key people. That policy had given the railroads tremendous power in state and local government affairs. Much as he liked free passes, Hubbell seems not to have objected to Cummins. Perhaps he knew it would not have done any good.

Hubbell usually was strict about collecting his interest and principal on loans. He took few chances. He had a soft spot in his heart, however, for relatives, no matter how remote the relationship might be.

In 1889, H. D. Booge of Topeka, Kans., wanted to borrow $15,000 at 8 per cent interest for an investment in old Mexico. Hubbell ordinarily would not have touched a proposition that far from home. Booge, however, was a "relative." Hubbell's sister Annie had married James E. Booge at Sioux City in about 1861. H. D. was James' brother.

Annie Hubbell Booge died in 1864. Even though 25 years had elapsed since Annie's death, and even though H. D. Booge had only been her brother-in-law in the first place, Hubbell cooperated with the Topeka man to an unusual extent. Hubbell wrote in his diary: "I promised to give him (Booge) a letter of credit on me for $250,000".

Few indeed were the persons who ever got Hubbell to give them a letter of credit for $250,000! The diary does not record how Hubbell came out on the Mexican venture.

Hubbell was always getting suggestions that he finance this or that group in a business venture. On November 18, 1913, for example, he wrote this in his diary: "W. B. Hanes suggested that G. S. Gilbertson, Emory English, L. C. Kurtz, E. T. Meredith, and T. J. Kelleher buy the American Life Ins. Company and that I loan to those men $100,000 at 8 per cent for 10 years." Hubbell decided a few days later not to make the loan.

Hubbell was not an inexhaustible source of money. Often he had to do large scale borrowing himself. As late as 1922 he personally borrowed $92,000 from the Iowa National Bank at 5 per cent. On April 2, 1914, he arranged over the phone "with Homer Miller for $25,000 or $30,000 at 4 per cent on call." Hubbell needed the money to pay taxes.

On January 2, 1909, he listed his debts at $502,101. The largest item was $224,656 that he owed his daughter, Beulah. Next largest was a $115,000 debt to the Equitable of New York. He also owed the St. Louis Union Trust Co., $41,774, the Metropolitan Trust Co., $20,500 and "Ida Reigelman" $10,000.

On the other hand, Hubbell sometimes was so well heeled that he had trouble finding safe places in which to invest his money. After sale of the Fonda and Boone lines to the Milwaukee railroad in 1898, he wrote in his diary January 16, 1899: "Deposited a million dollars for three months in Park Bank New York. 2% interest rate."

He wasn't very happy with that interest yield. But that was all he could get at the moment in New York. He also deposited $250,000 with the Metropolitan Trust Co., in New York at 2 per cent on call. He asked the Metropolitan if the interest rate would be increased if he boosted his deposit above $300,000. The company's answer is not recorded. He often borrowed large sums from Metropolitan, however, and the company might have agreed to pay more interest temporarily to a good customer.

Not all his deals were large, nor did they always involve "big name" people. In 1908 he went into the Valley National Bank and endorsed a $2,500 note for "Carrie C. Lindholm and her father S. J. Lindholm."

"She will use this money to buy 80 acres of land in Oregon which is improved with an apple and peach orchard," Hubbell wrote. "She has a house and lot in Seattle which rents for $40 a month. She expects to sell this house and lot and with the proceeds pay the note at the bank within six months."

Hubbell often didn't give that much space in his diary to a half-a-million dollar railroad transaction.

The diary discloses that an unnamed Des Moines bank came close to ceasing business in 1893 because of involvement with the streetcar company. Jefferson Polk operated the streetcar lines. At this time Polk was not friendly with Hubbell, his former partner. The bank held some streetcar notes. Hubbell was financially interested in the bank in question.

"After hearing about the condition of the street railway, it was concluded that Mr. Hunter should demand immediately the endorsement of Mr. Polk on the paper," the diary says under date of August 8, 1893.

"If that could not be had, then we would demand bonds."

The next day Hubbell served notice that "if we did not get the street railway papers secured, that we ought to put the bank into liquidation at once." Polk (or somebody) came through. Hubbell got word next day that $51,000 in bonds had been posted as security.

Hubbell had two complaints to make about Des Moines banks. He didn't like the high salaries some of the bankers collected. And he was unhappy over the fact that he was unable to get himself elected to the board of directors of certain banks in which he held a sizable stock interest.

On September 5, 1905, he wrote: "I went to the Des Moines National Bank. I told Reynolds that we earnestly protested that his salary should be reduced. That I wanted to consolidate with some bank. Two, I wanted to sell out our stock. Three, wanted to buy him out. Four, wanted to liquidate. This last angered him somewhat." The diary does not say whether Reynolds' salary was reduced.

In 1910, the Capitol City State Bank had 1,000 shares outstanding. Hubbell was the principal stockholder, with 200 shares. In that same year, he also owned 42 shares out of 500 in the Home Savings Bank. By 1912, he had increased his holdings in Capitol City to 494 shares. Even so, he could not get on the Capitol City board of directors at the 1915 meeting.

"I could not be elected," the diary says. "I asked the reason why and (J. A.) McKinney said they were afraid of me."

Hubbell tried again in 1916 and 1918 at Capitol City, failed both times. In 1916 he voted his stock for James L. Callanan as director but Callanan could not win either. At one point in the argument, Hubbell refused $100,000 for his Capitol City stock.

Hubbell was disappointed at not being elected a director. But he was always philosophical about such things. More painful to him were actual business losses. For example, he quite understandably was unhappy when rental property stood vacant for several weeks. He kept close track of such things. On March 28, 1908, he reported sadly: "Losing rents at rate per annum $7,836."

Such a vacancy loss really was not of vital importance considering the scope of his real estate operations. The diary contains an occasional overall report on rents. In the year 1925, for example, the net rents for F. M. Hubbell, Son & Company, Incorporated were $242,865; for the Hubbell Estate, $300,010.

How would Hubbell have fared if he had started out in 1855 with 1955 taxes to pay? Would he have been able to accumulate great wealth if he had had to pay federal income taxes at present-day rates?

There is no question but that modern taxes would have slowed him down considerably. Nevertheless, he undoubtedly would have become a rich man anyway. A large part of his wealth resulted from big increases in the value of his property. He didn't pay much for most of his property in "Factory Addition," for example. That section was low and marshy and not considered of any real value at the time he bought it. Look at it today!

Also, the value of his railroad holdings, his insurance stock and his waterworks property all increased substantially in his lifetime. Such increases are taxable as "capital gains" at a rate of 25 per cent, much less than the rates assessed on the yearly earnings of high-income individuals.

Frederick M. Hubbell would have been an outstandingly successful businessman in any generation.

FREDERICK M. HUBBELL at about 75 years of age.

FREDERICK M. HUBBELL with his great grandchildren in 1927. Left to right: HELEN ANN HUBBELL, FREDERICK W. HUBBELL, JR., CRAWFORD C. HUBBELL, JAMES W. HUBBELL, JR., and MARY W. HUBBELL.

21

An Old Man

THERE WAS A lonely grandeur about Fred Hubbell as his powers ebbed with the passing years.

He was 85 years old in 1924. Management of his vast holdings by this time had passed into younger hands. His usefulness grew less and less. Yet he had few regrets. As a matter of fact, he did little regretting and complaining at any stage of his long life.

He appears to have decided early that being unhappy and railing against fate were a waste of time and energy. If he suffered a defeat, he usually was able to wipe that memory from his mind immediately and to concentrate his energies on the next battle.

"I am glad that I have lived without personal enmities and that I have been able to take the ups and downs of an active career without feeling personal bitterness," he once said. "There are some things that others do not do that I feel they ought to do but I have cultivated a philosophy for that."

As an old man, he continued to putter around his office. He checked the cash book each day (and put a dot after each entry). Occasionally he would put on

223

his hard derby hat and go out and personally do some collecting. Every month he visited a garage worker across the street and collected $20.00. (The worker was buying property on time and Hubbell did the financing.) The worker got a big kick out of the millionaire's regular visits to collect $20.

As age advanced, Hubbell's values inevitably changed. Railroads, banks, property, millions of dollars, all such things were not so important. What he wanted most of all now was for someone to come to see him. Preferably his sons, grandsons or great grandchildren. And he wanted Elmer Nelson, the family chauffeur, to take him out riding, always on Avenue Frederick M. Hubbell. But Elmer frequently was too busy.

Newspaper reporters often called at his house. He gladly let them in. They wanted to know his formula for success. Here is what he said on one occasion: "I suppose you would like to be a millionaire and I can tell you how to become one. Only four requisites are necessary. First, economy. If you are not economical and spend all the money you get hold of, you cannot become wealthy. Second, industry. If you are lazy and do not work, it doesn't make any difference how economical and stingy you are, you won't have anything Third, good health. If you are sick and the doctor wants to see you every day and give you medicine, you are handicapped and cannot make the grade.

"With these three requisites you will, in a reasonable time, have $1,000. The only other requisite is brains. I mean by that you have to have intellect enough to invest that $1,000 and not lose it. Economy, industry, good health and brains will make anybody rich. Some day you will have money to lend."

On another occasion, he said that a man "with an economical wife has far greater opportunity for financial success than the man whose wife wants to keep up with the Joneses."

"I had a wife who shared my plans for economy and thrift," he observed. "We had 60 years of happy married life before she left me last spring."

The diary for May 11, 1924, says: "Today just about noon Frances E. Hubbell, my wife, passed away. We were married March 11, 1863, so have lived together over 61 years. She was a good wife and I shall mourn her as long as I live."

Although he clung stubbornly to life for six more years, 1924 really was the beginning of the end of activity for Fred Hubbell. "I have about concluded to slow up on work," he wrote January 8. "I have told Jim to open the Trustees' mail." (That was a task he always had performed himself each morning.)

A long siege of illness started January 18. On that day he wrote: "Jim Hubbell says that I went down to the Equitable and attended a meeting of the loan committee. I cannot remember and thought I did not go out today."

For the next three months he did not leave Terrace Hill and scarcely got out of bed. The diary, which for decades had been filled with accounts of big bond issues, of important conferences in New York and Chicago, of high finance in Des Moines, was much briefer now. On February 11, all he wrote was: "F. W. Hubbell called this morning with his little boy. I was glad to see them."

On March 3, his diary consists of this: "A cloudy, gloomy day. It snowed for about half an hour this morning very hard. Spent the day reading. The snow covers the lawn and it looks white." On March 7, he wrote: "The lawn is covered with snow. I am feeling as well as usual. Gave $20 to a man whose house burned up a short time ago. He is a working man and has four children."

On March 8, he went downstairs in his home for the first time since January 17, "almost two months." On April 14, "I took a ride on Ave. Frederick Hubbell this afternoon." Elmer took him out in the Essex coupe.

The old man was more or less at Elmer's mercy. "Elmer wanted today for himself so I did not leave Terrace Hill," Hubbell wrote July 4. "No one called on me."

When he was well, he had periods of activity, however. In 1925 "I was admitted as a member of the Episcopal church." One afternoon in 1927 "my great grandchildren called on me this afternoon and had their pictures taken. We had a lively time."

On September 17, 1924, he "took dinner at Hotel Fort Des Moines in honor of John W. Davis, Dem., candidate for president." But on October 8, he wrote: "It is raining today. I did not get to the office until 10:30 a.m. Did not go to the (Des Moines) club today. I think I will stop going. It is better for me to sleep."

Henry C. Wallace, secretary of agriculture under President Harding, died in October. He was a resident of Des Moines. Hubbell wrote on October 29: "Henry C. Wallace funeral today at 2 p.m. I was unable to attend the funeral as Elmer was so busy waiting on other people I could not get him to wait on me."

On November 4, Fred was able to go to the polls. ("Voted early, a Democratic ticket," he reported. He was a Democrat all his life.)

He was very interested in how much longer he had to live. On November 21, 1924, he reported. "I inquired of the Equitable what was the expectation of life for a man almost 86 years old, and was told 3½ years. So if I do not reach the age of 89½ years I shall not have had a fair count." (He lived almost 5 more years.)

He went to the Des Moines Club to drink tea on January 17, 1925, his 86th birthday. "Everyone I meet congratulates me on my age," he proudly reported. But on February 4, he sadly wrote: "J. W. Hubbell wants me to stop buying real estate in Des Moines, and I have agreed to stop."

The chauffeur situation did not improve. On February 13, Hubbell wrote that "I don't think I can get a ride as Elmer is so busy taking care of the younger Hubbells that I can't get him to take me home at 4 p.m."

On April 13, David Kirk, a 13-year-old boy, had his bicycle stolen. "I sent for him to come and see me and gave him $10," the diary says. "Asked him to come back and see me some time."

At the same time, Hubbell did not consider himself all washed up. On June 25 he "rode to the end of Avenue Frederick Hubbell (and) made up my mind to extend Avenue Frederick Hubbell to Bondurant."

On August 3, he gave $1,000 to the children's home. On September 4, he happily reported: "Mrs. James W. Hubbell gave birth this morning to a son. My great grandson. I sent her a check for $1,000 and asked her to name the boy Frederick Marion Hubbell." But that was not to be. The child had already been named Crawford Cox Hubbell. "They tell me that I will have to wait until another boy is born before I can have one named after me," Hubbell wrote.

On November 5, he went to the office and found interstate commerce commission agents examining the books of the Des Moines Terminal Co. "They have taken my office and I have no place to stay," he reported. He went home.

Sickness again engulfed him in the winter of 1925-1926. This siege lasted for months. Again his fondest wish was for callers. The January 21, 1926, diary says: "F. C. H. (Fred C. Hubbell, his oldest son) called on me. He calls every day. I am trying to have all the Hubbells call with some regularity."

On February 1, he wrote: "It is a cloudy day. I am sitting up watching the squirrels have a good time. Am as well as I was yesterday but not very strong. Nobody has called except the doctor."

On February 15, he observed that he had been confined to the house 74 consecutive days and "I am awfully tired of it." On February 21, he wrote that "the Hubbells have all left town except James W. H. I hope he will call and see me today. Well, he did call today and it was the only call I had."

One highlight of his last years took place on July 27, 1929. Back in 1878, he had been the first Des Moines resident to install a telephone connection between his home and his office.

In 1929, the first dial telephone was installed in Des Moines, again connecting Hubbell's home with his office. The span of time between the two events was

51 years. With the aid of a telephone company official, Fred Hubbell dialed 3-3228. (Still the Hubbell office number, incidentally.)

"Hello. Is that you Grover?" he said into the telephone. Grover C. Hubbell was in the office at the other end. "Pretty good," Hubbell said after he had hung up. "Fifty years ago we would have said this was impossible. Today I've done it."

His long diary, started when he was a 15-year-old boy, came to an end December 23, 1927. The last entry says only this: "I did not go to the office today. Stayed at home."

He wrote nothing after that.

Death came to Frederick Marion Hubbell at 5 o'clock in the morning of November 11, 1930. His age, as he himself would have recorded it in his diary, was "91 years, 9 months, 3 weeks and 5 days."

He is buried in the family mausoleum in Woodland Cemetery, Des Moines, with his wife and his son, Fred C. Also in the same cemetery are Jefferson Polk, Albert B. Cummins, Hoyt Sherman, Lampson Sherman, DeVere Thompson, Phineas Casady, Wesley Redhead, General Crocker and many others who were associates, rivals and friends of Frederick M. Hubbell during his long lifetime. In death, their final resting places all are within a few hundred feet of each other in Woodland.

22

1955

DES MOINES IS a city of 180,000 now, more than 100 times bigger than the village of 1,500 first seen a century ago by the longhaired boy with the big bow tie..

If Fred Hubbell were to return today, he probably would not be too surprised at the continued growth of the city. He knew Des Moines would prosper. In 1925, he said: "If I were 22 years old today, I would again settle in Des Moines. I would work and save and invest in Des Moines real estate because I know that in ten years it would make me a lot of money."

A 1925 newspaper editorial commented: "Mr. Hubbell engaged in many enterprises but he never lost sight of downtown Des Moines real estate . . . There have been all sorts of ups and downs in his time but he has demonstrated (the value of) sticking to one place, studying one thing . . . Mr. Hubbell has spent money where he made it. Every dollar goes back into Des Moines investment. Mr. Hubbell belongs to Des Moines . . . Just how much he has meant to the city nobody can estimate."

There are evidences everywhere in present-day Des Moines of Hubbell faith in the city's long range possibilities. Prominent in the Des Moines skyline are the Equitable Building, the Hubbell Building, the Kirkwood Hotel, the west half of the Younker Store, the Victoria Hotel, Terrace Hill, and other past or present Hubbell landmarks.

Many other major Des Moines buildings stand on Hubbell-owned land. These include the Farm Bureau Building, the Insurance Exchange Building, the Des Moines Club, the Paramount Theater Building, the Troy Laundry and Cascade Laundries. The Hubbells also own part of the site of the Jewett Building. The original lease for that site was made back in 1886 by Frederick M. Hubbell himself.

About 75 per cent of Des Moines' "Factory Addition" is Hubbell property. This big industrial tract immediately south of downtown Des Moines extends in general from Vine Street south to the Raccoon River and from about Twelfth Street east to Third Street. On these 112 Hubbell acres are located such well-known firms as Pittsburgh-Des Moines Steel Company, Des Moines Steel Company, New Monarch Machine & Stamping Company, Carr & Moehl Company, John Deere Plow Co. of Moline, Iowa Concrete Block & Material Company, Crown Concrete Company, Consumers Cooperative Assn., Grocers Wholesale Co-op, Inc., and dozens of others.

Much of the present-day Hubbell property dates far back in Des Moines history. Frederick M. Hubbell acquired a large part of Factory Addition before 1888. There is good reason to believe he bought some of it in the 1860s and 1870s.

The Hubbell Interests have hundreds of tenants on their rent rolls. They are exceedingly proud of the splendid landlord-tenant relationship which has existed for many years. The following tenants have occupied Hubbell property for 25 years or longer:

Name of Company	Year of First Lease
Carr & Moehl Company	1899
Des Moines Union Railway Company	1899
Pittsburgh-Des Moines Steel Company	1900
Stoner McCray System	1901
Western Newspaper Union	1904
Des Moines Nursery Company	1905
Pratt Paper Company	1909
Des Moines Club	1910
Lagerquist Body Company	1910
Troy Laundry Company	1910
Sherman Paper Stock Company	1912
Union Carbide & Carbon Corp.	1912
Aetna Life Insurance Company	1913
Brooks & Borg	1913
Fort Dodge, Des Moines & Southern Railway Company	1913

Hawkeye Marquette Cement Company........1913
Home Loan & Investment Company...............1913
Iowa Mutual Tornado Insurance
    Association 1913
Arthur H. Neumann & Bros....................1913
Town Mutual Dwelling Insurance
    Company 1913
Cushman Wilson Oil Company................1914
Underwood Corporation 1914
New Monarch Machine & Stamping
    Company 1916
Des Moines Steel Company......................1917
Garmer & Stiles Company.......................1918
Cascade Laundry Company.....................1919
Elaterite Paint & Mfg. Co.......................1919
Portland Cement Association..................1919
Schulze Baking Company........................1919
Kewanee Boiler Company........................1920
Insurance Exchange Building..................1920
Jacob Schmidt Brewing Company..........1920
Chicago Great Western Railroad.............1921
Electric Equipment Company,
    Incorporated 1921
Jewett Lumber Company.........................1921
Leachman Lumber Company...................1921
Sinclair Refining Company......................1921
Cities Service Oil Company.....................1922
The Commonwealth Company................1922

Superior Oil Company.................................1922
Furlong & Baker Electric Company.................1923
Wm. Knudson & Sons, Inc.........................1923
A. Y. McDonald Mfg. Co..........................1923
Root Casket Company.............................1923
The Simmons Company............................1923
Tanvilac Company, Incorporated..................1923
Universal Film Exchange.........................1923
M. A. Wolin Plumbing & Heating
    Company 1923
Younker Bros., Inc..............................1923
Hughes Barber Shop.............................1924
Carpenter Oil Company..........................1925
Potthoff & Rosene Company......................1925
Standard Chemical Company......................1925
Victoria Hotel Company.........................1925
Great Atlantic & Pacific Tea Company.........1926
Lovejoy Construction Company...................1926
Arnold Schaetzle, Attorney.....................1926
The Texas Company 1926
C. J. Trawver..................................1926
Twentieth Century-Fox Film Corporation...1926
United Des Moines Clay Company.................1926
Brown Garage Company...........................1927
Erie Railway...................................1927
Wm. H. Metz & Company..........................1927
Mid-Continent Petroleum Corp...................1927

O'Dea Chevrolet Company............................1927
Thomas Electric Company..........................1927
Richards Wilcox Mfg. Co............................1927
John Deere Plow Co. of Moline................1928
Furlong Machine Company........................1928
Sloan Pierce Lumber Company................1928
Iowa Radio Corporation............................1929
Phillips Petroleum Company....................1929
Ceco Steel Products Corporation..............1930
Des Moines Waste Paper Company............1930
Grocers Wholesale Company......................1930
Kirkwood Hotel (Tangney-McGinn,
    Inc.) 1930
Warner Bros. Pict. Dist. Corp....................1930

The real estate taxes paid to the Polk County Treasurer's Office each year on Hubbell properties exceed $750,000.

Much bigger now than the Hubbell real estate holdings is the Equitable Life Insurance Company of Iowa. Far-seeing though he was, Fred Hubbell never had any idea that the company one day would have more than one billion three hundred million dollars of insurance in force. The Equitable is a decided asset to Des Moines. The payroll for the company's 500 Des Moines employees is $2,160,000 a year.

Frederick M. Hubbell was not a person who allowed other individuals to make his decisions. He wanted that power and that right centered in himself most of the time. Yet, he could find little cause to complain in the record made by the Hubbells since he stepped down from active management 30 or more years ago.

His descendants have proved to be able, industrious and imaginative, even into the fourth generation. As the courts would say, at present there are 44 living heirs "to the body of Frederick M. Hubbell."

At the family helm are the three living trustees of the F. M. Hubbell Estate. They are Grover C. Hubbell, 72; Frederick Windsor Hubbell, 63; and James Windsor Hubbell, 59. Grover is a son of F. M., Frederick and James are grandsons. They are sons of the late Frederick C. Hubbell.

Countess Beulah Cooper Hubbell Wachtmeister, 80, is a daughter of F. M. Hubbell. She lives in Paris.

Surviving Frederick M. Hubbell at the present time are one son and one daughter (Grover and Countess Wachtmeister), three grandsons and three granddaughters, 18 great grandchildren and 18 great great grandchildren.

Frederick Windsor Hubbell is President of the Equitable. Grover Hubbell is a Vice-President and James Windsor Hubbell is Secretary-Treasurer. James W. also is Chairman of the Board of the Bankers Trust Company, and is President of F. M. Hubbell, Son & Company, Incorporated, the Des Moines Terminal

Company and Hubbell, Inc. Frederick W. Hubbell also heads Hubbell Brothers, Inc. All the Trustees are officers in the various enterprises.

The Hubbells are substantial participants in civic and hospital drives and in Drake University programs. Grover C. Hubbell was winner of The Des Moines Tribune's Community Service Award in 1948.

In the Hubbell Building at Ninth and Walnut Streets are centered many of the companies which provide overall guidance of Hubbell interests. This is the building where Frederick M. had his high desk and where he checked the cash book each day. Offices of the Hubbell Estate, F. M. Hubbell, Son & Company, Incorporated, Grover C. Hubbell and James W. Hubbell are located in the same building.

The Hubbell Realty Company, headed by Simpson P. Smith, is located in the Hubbell Building. So are the offices of The Thompson Trust, the Des Moines Terminal Company and most of the 17 enterprises in which members of the Hubbell family figure.

What will happen to all this property as time inevitably rolls on? All man-made instruments come to an end. The time will come when the F. M. Hubbell Estate will be liquidated according to law and will be no more. But that time probably won't be reached until the latter years of the present century.

Aerial view of Des Moines looking northwest. Raccoon River is lower left, Des Moines River is at right.

It seems fantastic that this setup all dates back to
a small but determined boy who came west with his
father 100 years ago to buy cheap land in early Iowa.
Such things could happen only in a vigorous and growing nation with a free economy. Hubbell's spectacular
success is a lasting monument to the wave of pioneers
who moved into this empty but promising land long
ago.

The late J. B. Weaver, Des Moines attorney and
poet, sensed this pioneer urge. In 1909, Des Moines
leaders gave a party honoring Frederick M. Hubbell
on his 70th birthday. Weaver wrote some verse for
the occasion, addressed to Hubbell. Here was the last
stanza:

> *"You answered, thousands by your side,*
>   *"Strong builders of the west.*
> *"Through 70 years of toil and joy*
>   *"You met each hardy test.*
> *"Ah, boy, if only we might hear*
>   *"Amidst our city's roar*
> *"The same clear empire-building call*
>   *"That came to you of yore."*

PROGENY OF THE FREDERICK M. HUBBELL FAMILY*

FREDERICK MARION HUBBELL

b. Jan. 17, 1839
d. Nov. 11, 1930

1. Frederick Cooper Hubbell
   b. April 29, 1864
   d. May 3, 1947

2. Beulah C. Hubbell Wachtmeister
   b. July 5, 1874
   d. January 16, 1958

3. Grover Cooper Hubbell
   b. Feb. 3, 1883
   d. Dec. 9, 1956

( ) Denotes living heirs to body of F. M. Hubbell per stirpes
56 living heirs to body of F. M. Hubbell
*Updated as of July 1, 1964

240

FREDERICK COOPER HUBBELL
(22)

1. **Frederick Windsor Hubbell**
   b. Nov. 24, 1891
   d. Mar. 13, 1959

   1. Frederick Windsor Hubbell, Jr.
      b. June 17, 1921
      d. May 29, 1936

   2. Helen Ann Hubbell Ingham
      b. Sept. 13, 1924

      1. Richard Schuyler Ingham, Jr.
         b. Oct. 7, 1945
      2. Helen Annelle Ingham
         b. Aug. 30, 1947
      3. Hilary Frances Ingham
         b. May 24, 1950
      4. Sharon Clark Ingham
         b. Nov. 25, 1951
      5. Frederick Hubbell Ingham
         b. Sept. 22, 1958

2. **James Windsor Hubbell**
   b. June 5, 1895
   d. Nov. 17, 1962

   1. James Windsor Hubbell, Jr.
      b. May 17, 1922

      1. James Windsor Hubbell, III
         b. June 10, 1948
      2. Harriet Houx Hubbell
         b. Sept. 16, 1949
      3. Frederick Shelton Hubbell
         b. April 25, 1951
      4. Michael Cooper Hubbell
         b. Aug. 21, 1953

   2. Mary Windsor Hubbell Waterman
      b. Dec. 25, 1923

      1. Larned Allen Waterman, Jr.
         b. Aug. 14, 1945
      2. Mary Windsor Waterman
         b. June 7, 1947
      3. Ann Elisabeth Waterman
         b. May 31, 1949
      4. Lynn Waterman
         b. July 9, 1950
      5. Leslie Hubbell Waterman
         b. Aug. 13, 1952

   3. Crawford Cox Hubbell
      b. Sept. 4, 1925

      1. Christopher Hubbell
         b. Nov. 3, 1951
      2. Carol Mallen Hubbell
         b. Jan. 25, 1954
      3. Catherine Windsor Hubbell
         b. Mar. 6, 1956
      4. Crawford Cox Hubbell, Jr.
         b. Jan. 4, 1958

241

BEULAH HUBBELL
WACHTMEISTER
(7)

1. Fredrik Hans Carl
   Wachtmeister
   b. April 27, 1909

   1. Marianne Brita
      Wachtmeister Adair
      b. Aug. 29, 1935

      1. Robert Fredrik Martin Adair
         b. Nov. 2, 1956

      2. Catherine Marianne Adair
         b. Oct. 14, 1958

   2. Hans Fredrik Edward
      Wachtmeister
      b. Nov. 1, 1944

   3. Edward Carl Axel
      Wachtmeister
      b. May 21, 1947

   4. Linda Elisabeth Anne
      Wachtmeister
      b. March 9, 1950

GROVER COOPER HUBBELL
(26)

1. Frances Cooper Hubbell Ingham
b. Oct. 18, 1906

  1. Patricia Ingham Davis
     b. March 17, 1934

     1. Stephen Everett Davis
        b. April 6, 1953
     2. Frances Elizabeth Davis
        b. May 28, 1955
     3. Anna Patricia Davis
        b. Dec. 7, 1957
     4. Frederick Godfrey Davis
        b. Dec. 6, 1959

  2. Hepburn Ingham, Jr.
     b. Feb. 15, 1936

     1. Mark Grover Ingham
        b. Jan. 6, 1957
     2. Hepburn Ingham, III
        b. July 10, 1958
     3. Valerie Ingham
        b. Nov. 4, 1959
     4. Stewart Ingham
        b. April 18, 1962

  3. Carl Frederick Ingham
     b. Dec. 25, 1937

     1. Suzanne Ingham
        b. March 7, 1962

  4. Hubbell Ingham
     b. June 28, 1941

2. Helen Virginia Hubbell Thorne Barshell
b. Feb. 12, 1908

  1. Anne Godfrey Thorne Weaver
     b. May 17, 1933

     1. Wendy Anne Weaver
        b. March 16, 1953
     2. James McLaughlin Weaver
        b. Nov. 27, 1954
     3. Philip Thorne Weaver
        b. Dec. 31, 1956
     4. Laura Ann Weaver
        b. June 18, 1964

  2. Helen Virginia Barshell
     b. Sept. 8, 1945

  3. Leslie Jane Barshell
     b. Jan. 27, 1947

3. Mary Belle Hubbell Windsor
b. Dec. 15, 1911

  1. James Harvey Windsor, III
     b. Jan. 19, 1933

     1. James Harvey Windsor, IV
        b. Oct. 18, 1959

  2. Grover Hubbell Windsor
     b. Aug. 20, 1934

  3. William Raymond Windsor
     b. April 21, 1938

243

Epilogue 1988

As MUST HAPPEN to all men and man-made institutions, the Hubbell Trust, holding the fortune amassed by Frederick M. Hubbell, expired November 17, 1983. The next day trust assets of more than $200 million were distributed to his thirteen heirs. The distribution brought an end to what might be called the extended life of F. M. Hubbell, who died at 91 years of age in 1930. But he exercised considerable control, through the trust he created, for nearly a half-century following his death. The trust assets represented a value of more than 40 million times greater than the lone $5 gold piece he possessed when he took his first job as a sixteen-year-old in Des Moines in 1855.

Demise of the trust was no sudden decision. Iowa law decrees that a trust may not exist longer than twenty-one years beyond the death of the final survivor named to the original board of trustees. Grandson James W. Hubbell was that survivor. He died November 17, 1962.

The principal leadership burden in liquidating the trust fell upon the shoulders of James W. Hubbell, Jr., 66, known to family and friends as Jim. As board chairman of the parent Equitable and one of the estate's final trustees, he has long been a key force in the Hubbell empire.

One of Jim Hubbell's principal legal tasks in ending the trust was to prove to the courts the deaths of at least nine family members in the preceding 53 years. This he did by presenting certificates of the deaths of the five original trustees: F. M. Hubbell in 1930, Frederick C. Hubbell in 1947, Grover Hubbell in 1956, Frederick W. Hubbell in 1959, and J. W. Hubbell in 1962. Then it was also necessary to prove other deaths to establish the inheritance rights of family members still living. These proofs included the deaths of Frederick W. Hubbell, Jr., in 1936; Beulah Hubbell Wachtmeister (in Paris) in 1958; and Fredrik

245

Hans Carl Wachtmeister and Virginia Hubbell Barshell, both in 1973.

Granddaughter Frances Hubbell Ingham died at 81 years of age in 1988. She drew considerable notice in 1980 when she was listed in Iowa as the vice-presidential candidate in John Anderson's independent race for president.

In granting court approval of dissolution of the trust, District Judge Ray Hanrahan said laconically, "This matter is closed." Present in Des Moines for the historic occasion were all thirteen heirs and approximately eighty members of their families. They came from around the nation and from England as well.

The heirs received their respective shares of the trust at a gala luncheon party at Wakonda Country Club in Des Moines. The largest share, one-sixth of the total, went to great-granddaughter Helen Hubbell Ingham of Fort Lauderdale, Fla. The value of her portion was estimated at $34 million and was the largest because she was the only survivor in her line of the family.

The smallest shares, one twenty-seventh apiece, went to three other great-granddaughters: Anne Thorne Weaver of Omaha, Neb.; Helen B. Nemacheck of Thienville, Wis.; and Leslie B. Coleman of Littleton, Colo.—approximately $7.5 million each.

Granddaughters Frances Ingham and Mary Belle Windsor of Des Moines each received one-ninth. Shares of one-twelfth went to great-grandchildren Marianne W. Adair of Chobham, Surrey, England; Linda E. A. Wachtmeister of Seattle, Wash.; Edward C. Wachtmeister of Warrenton, Va.; and Hans F. E. Wachtmeister of Virginia Beach, Va. Great-grandchildren James W. Hubbell, Jr., of Des Moines, and Crawford C. Hubbell of Phoenix, Ariz., and Mary Waterman of Davenport, Ia., were each allocated one-eighteenth shares.

About two-thirds of the assets were shares of stock in the

Equitable of Iowa companies, of which the Equitable Life Insurance Company of Iowa is a part. The other third consisted mostly of stock in F. M. Hubbell, Son & Co., which had become a holding company for the extensive Hubbell property interests.

Though they had no access to the assets while the trust was still in force, the heirs drew incomes annually from the earnings. The last public report stated that the heirs received more than $6 million in earnings in 1982, the largest single share being more than $1 million and the smallest more than $220,000.

There were no family squabbles as the curtain rang down on the trust. "It all ended with everybody talking to everybody as friends and we'll remain friends," said Jim. "That was the primary goal of our planning." All too often the process of dividing up estates can lead to bitterness that lasts a lifetime. Family members gathered in Des Moines annually for some years before the end of the trust to receive business reports. Those meetings have continued since.

The heirs acquired their proportionate shares without having to pay federal income taxes. As they took title to their assets, however, they assumed the cost basis of those assets for future tax purposes, under one dollar a share in the case of Equitable stock. The heirs then became liable for tax if and when they sold the securities or gave them to relatives such as their children. And, of course, estates are taxable after death.

Jim Hubbell always greatly admired the accomplishments of his great-grandfather. Jim once said, "In effect, since there were no income tax laws in 1903 (when the trust was set up), Frederick M. Hubbell succeeded in passing his wealth through several generations of his family tax-free. A unique trust? Yes. A successful trust? Yes. F. M. would have been pleased with the results."

It is highly likely that F. M. Hubbell would have given his approval to the changes made through the courts in the policies he enunciated in the trust indenture. He was among the first of his time to sense new economic trends and to alter his policies to take advantage of them.

F. M. might have been surprised, however, at some of the trust's changes in direction, such as the sale in 1972 of 750,000 shares of Equitable stock to the general public. That, of course, was against his policy of always buying and never selling Equitable stock, with the result that he ultimately got it all. As the expiration of the trust approached, however, it became necessary to acquire a yardstick of value and a market for the stock. Otherwise the heirs ultimately would have no reliable way of judging its worth, nor would they be able to sell it conveniently at a fair price. Thus the decision was made to make a public offering of the 750,000 shares, 15 percent of the five million shares in the trust and in other Hubbell hands. Both the trust and family members allocated 15 percent of their holdings to the sale. The issuing price was $24 a share and it has fluctuated widely since then, from a high of around $27 to a low of about $10 in the 1970s when all stocks plummeted.

The move to go public with Equitable grew out of a study of the Hubbell structure by a crack eastern legal team headed by James Casner, Harvard law dean. The fifteen-month study in 1968–1969 resulted in an analysis and set of recommendations that filled ten loose-leaf volumes.

In addition to the stock sale, the team recommended that court permission be sought to sell any or all the Class A real property. But Mr. Hubbell had decreed that none of that be sold during the life of the trust. "The restriction severely limited the trustees' ability to manage the real estate profitably for the beneficiaries," said Jim Hubbell. "The lack of any instructions for the properties after the trust's termination likewise severely limited the market value of the many properties."

The courts agreed in 1969 that the Class A restriction no longer was a good idea and lifted the ban. The trustees thereupon sold 38 parcels in the next three and a half years for more than $2.9 million. It was in accordance with another team recommendation that F. M. Hubbell, Son & Co., was made into a holding company for real estate and other assets.

Aging Terrace Hill proved to be a special Class A "not-to-be-sold" problem. The old home had been occupied only by caretakers after Anna Hubbell moved out in 1957 following the 1956 death of her husband Grover. None of the other Hubbells wanted to live there. It was a costly maintenance and tax situation for the trust and promised to become more so with the approaching sizable expenditures for needed rehabilitation of the century-old building.

Two events became part of the emotional tradition of Terrace Hill in the final generation of the trust. The first occurred in April 1957 when Anna Hubbell walked out the big front door, leaving Terrace Hill without a resident Hubbell for the first time in nearly 73 years. The second took place in December 1963 when empty Terrace Hill came to life with a swinging party honoring Anna on her 80th birthday. She was still a beautiful woman and active as well. She danced with her grandsons and was as light on her feet as they were on theirs.

The Hubbells gathered from far and near for that party, including grandson Fredrick Hans Carl Wachtmeister, then 54, of Warrenton, Va. He had had a lot of fun as a child sliding down the bannisters of the famed Terrace Hill staircase. He did some more sliding for the benefit of photographers at Anna's party.

Acting upon another recommendation of the analysis team, the trustees asked for authority to transfer Terrace Hill to the heirs with a view to donating it to a public use. The courts in 1971 approved sale of the home to the heirs for $263,000. They then gave the home on its eight-acre site to the State of Iowa for use as the governor's mansion.

The state spent more than $3 million in private donations and appropriations, restoring the home and carriage house and constructing a modern apartment on the third floor. Governor Robert Ray and his family were the first occupants. In 1976, they moved in and were followed in 1983 by Governor Terry Branstad and his family.

Terrace Hill, which has been called an architectural Rembrandt, has become a top visitors' attraction in Des Moines as well as a place for major official state and sometimes private functions.

All the Hubbells explored Terrace Hill the weekend after the trust expired. They saw first-hand the remodeled historic surroundings where the patriarch of the family lived for 46 years before his death.

Perhaps the most startling business development in the final years of the trust was the 1979 purchase by the Equitable of the Younkers department store chain, with headquarters in Des Moines. The reported purchase price was $73 million, one of the biggest business deals in Des Moines history. The intense competition in the retail field led Younkers to broaden its base in 1987 by buying and absorbing the Brandeis store chain, which had its headquarters in Omaha.

The Hubbell presence continued strong in Des Moines in 1988, both socially and economically. Fifth-generation Hubbells were assuming top business posts. Frederick S., 37, was president of the parent Equitable. James III, 40, was president and Michael C., 34, vice president of Hubbell Realty. Assets of Equitable insurance reached a company record level of $1.7 billion. Extensive property interests included principal ownership of the new $50 million downtown Kaleidoscope office building and the new $11 million Capitol Center near the statehouse, as well as the wholly owned $10 million Locust Street Mall and parking garage. These properties were in addition to the long-held Equitable, Hubbell, and Younkers buildings and the large factory addition south of the loop, which has been renamed River Point. Other possessions included dozens of smaller pieces of Des Moines real estate, an office building in Minneapolis, and another in Fort Dodge.

A Hubbell family story heard for the first time in recent years dates back to the nineteenth century. It centers around Mary Wilkins, who jilted young Frederick M. Hubbell at Sioux City in the late 1850s, marrying Charles Rustin instead. Tradition has it that she had no children, that perhaps she could not do so. This prompted a modern-day Hubbell to say: "Isn't it lucky for us that grandfather didn't marry Mary Wilkins. None of us would be here today."

The Hubbell Trust probably would not have been born either. Frederick M. Hubbell would not have had any descendants for whom to preserve his wealth. And Des Moines history and tradition would have been the worse for it.

Sources

This biography is based on material obtained from the following sources:

Hubbell Daily Diaries 1855-56-57-58-81-82-83-84 and 1888 through 1927.

One large and one small "perpetual" diary.

Hubbell letterbooks and other papers in the offices of the Hubbell Estate, Hubbell Building, Des Moines.

Grenville Dodge papers, Iowa state historical department.

Files of The Des Moines Register and Tribune, The Des Moines Leader and The Des Moines Capital.

Files of The Sioux City Eagle.

Minutes of the Equitable Life Insurance Company of Iowa.

History of The Des Moines Waterworks and other waterworks information provided by Dale Maffitt.

"Historical Atlas of Iowa:" (Andreas.)

"The Story of Sioux County:" (Dyke.)

"The People of Iowa:" (Harlan.)

"History of Iowa:" (Gue.)

"Iowa: Its History and Its Foremost Citizens:" (Brigham.)

Corporate History of the Wabash Railroad.

"History of the Milwaukee Railroad:" (Field.)

"Des Moines Mail & Times:" souvenir book (1891.)

"Pioneers of Polk County:" (Andrews.)

"The History of Polk County, Iowa:" (1880.)

"The Palimpsest, 1932:" (publication of The State Historical Society of Iowa.)

"I Remember, I Remember:" (Cyrenus Cole.)

Personal interviews with Grover C. Hubbell, Frederick W. Hubbell, James W. Hubbell, Simpson Smith, R. S. Ruemper, Fred Bristol, Don Marshall, Emory English, Oscar Strauss, Eskil Carlson, Earl Smith and others.

W. Scott Reiniger translated shorthand in the Hubbell diaries.

Pictures are from the Hubbell family albums, the files of The Des Moines Register and Tribune and the state historical department.

The entire office staff of the Hubbell Estate provided invaluable help in putting this book together.

My wife, Mary, devoted many weeks of work to transcribing research notes and in helping classify the material. It would not have been possible to publish this volume in the allotted time without her tireless and faithful assistance.

GEORGE S. MILLS

Index

Adel, Iowa, 1
Aetna Life Insurance Company, 233
Albia, Iowa, 64, 72
Allen, B. F., 50, 59, 95-98, 118-119, 145, 171-172, 174
Allen, Frank, 130
Allen University, 173
Alliance Bank (England), 194
Allison, Senator William, 202
Alverson, H. C., 187-188
American Life Insurance Company, 217
Ames, Iowa, 64
Anderson, Mary, 190
Anderson, Ruth, 137
"Arabia" (Steamer), 17
Asbury M. E. Church, 51
Ashton, Iowa, 15, 199
Atlas of the World, 112
Austro - Hungarian Consulate (Chicago, Illinois), 180
Avenue Frederick M. Hubbell, 106, 144, 156-159, 167, 224, 226, 228

Bank of England, 194
Bankers Trust Company, 237
Barger, Miss, 111
Barshell, Helen Virginia Thorne, 140
Bechtel, Abbie, 112
Bell, Joseph, 52, 54
Birdseye, Isaac W., 120

Birmingham, Connecticut, 7
"Black Friday", 68
Blackstone (Law), 43-44, 48
Booge, Annie Hubbell, 217
    Also see Annie Hubbell
Booge, H. D., 87, 119-120, 217
Booge, James E., 87, 120, 217
Boone, Iowa, 64
Boone Standard, 76
Braden, John, 41
Brainard, 80
Brooks & Borg, 233
Brown Garage Company, 235
Brown, Harry, 114
Bryan, W. J., 203
"Burritt, F.", 120
Bush, L. H., 190
"Buzzard's Roost", 52-53
Caesar (Latin), 10
Callanan, James L., 66, 190, 221
Calliope, Iowa, 55
Camp Cody, 141
Capitol City State Bank, 220-221
Carpenter, Cyrus C., 66
Carpenter Oil Company, 235
Carr & Moehl Company, 232-233
Carroll, Governor (Iowa), 203
Cary, Robert, 180
Casady & Crocker, 48
Casady, Phineas M., 2, 9-13, 19, 21-22, 52, 57, 117, 119, 127, 190, 230

Casady, Simon, 190
Cascade Laundry Company, 232, 234
Cathell, Reverend J. Everist, 178
Ceco Steel Products Corporation, 236
Central National Bank, 107
Cerro Gordo County, Iowa, 83
Chase, Charley, 180
Chase, Ed, 188
Chicago Great Western Railroad, 234
Chicago, Milwaukee & St. Paul Railway Company, 89
Chicago Northwestern Railroad, 80
Cities Service Oil Company, 234
City Library (Des Moines, Iowa), 118
Clapp, E. R., 190
Clarkson, Dick, 213
Clarkson, J. S., 67, 73-74, 77, 81-82, 212-213
Cleveland, Grover, 202
Clive, Iowa, 71, 76
Cohen, Mr., 154
Cole, Judge C. C., 109
Cole, Chester C., 51
Cole, Cyrenus, 174
Colonial Wars Society, 191
Commonwealth Company, The, 234
Consumers Cooperative Association, 232
Cook County National Bank (Chicago, Illinois), 97
Cook, Dr. John K., 15
Cooper, Florence, 59
Cooper, Frances, 10, 14, 25, 37, 59, 100
    Also see Frances Cooper Hubbell
Cooper, Isaac, 10, 59, 100, 126
Cooper, James Fenimore, 10
Coulter, C. F., 112

Council Bluffs, Iowa, 15, 17, 64
Cowles, Gardner, 215
Cownie, John, 203
Craftsman School, 112
Crawford, W. M., 41
Crocker, Marcellus M., 14, 230
Crown Concrete Company, 232
Culver, Indiana, 132
Cummins, Albert B., 73, 79, 108-109, 188-189, 192, 215-216, 230
Currier (Lawyer), 44
Cushman Wilson Oil Company, 234
Dallas County, Iowa, 1, 11
Daly's Theater, 190
Davis, John W., 227
Dawson, Allten, 191
Denman, Augustus N., 79, 145, 152, 208
Denman, Charles, 147
Demoine House (Hotel), 13
Des Moines Albia & Knoxville Railroad, 72
Des Moines Capital (Newspaper), 144
Des Moines Chamber of Commerce, 106
Des Moines City Council, 144
Des Moines City Hall, 162
Des Moines Club, 113, 123, 168, 228, 232-233
Des Moines Coliseum, 112, 203
Des Moines College, 112
Des Moines Leader, 175, 212
Des Moines Life Insurance Company, 215
Des Moines & Minneapolis Railroad, 65, 67
Des Moines National Bank, 220
Des Moines Northern & Western Railway Co., 72, 86
Des Moines Northwestern Railroad, 71, 73, 79

Des Moines Nursery Company, 233

Des Moines & St. Louis Railroad Co., 72, 75, 85

Des Moines Savings Bank, 216

Des Moines State Journal, 10

Des Moines Steel Company, 232, 234

Des Moines Street Car Company, 103

Des Moines Terminal Company, 90-91, 229, 237-238

Des Moines Tribune, 159

Des Moines Tribune Community Service Award (1948), 238

Des Moines Union Railway Company, 64, 72, 74, 86, 89-92, 233

Des Moines Valley Railroad, 67

Des Moines Wastepaper Company, 236

Des Moines Water Company, 3, 58, 92, 110, 143, 145

Des Moines Water Supply Company, 145

Des Moines Waterworks Company, 145, 152-153

Des Moines Western Railway Company, 192

Dewey, Admiral George, 127

Dickinson, Matthew S., 12

Dodge, Grenville, 64, 67, 73-74, 79, 86, 127

Drake Medical School, 112

Drake University, 107, 112-113

Dry Creek, 55

Edmundsen, Dr., 129

Elaterite Paint & Manufacturing Company, 234

Electric Equipment Company, Incorporated, 234

Elliott, A. B., 157

Elliott, H. A., 188

"Emma" (Steamer), 17

English, Emory, 217

Episcopal Church, 227

Equitable Building, 118, 232

Equitable Life Insurance Company of Iowa, The, 2-3, 10, 50, 58, 92, 95, 100-101, 114, 117, 236

Equitable of London, 117

Equitable of New York, 218

Erie Railroad, 68, 235

Everett House (Hotel), 1-2

"Factory Addition", 58, 162, 222, 232-233

Fairweather, Tom, 144

Farm Bureau Building, 232

Federal Courthouse, 162

Federal Government Liberty Bonds, 106

Ferber, Edna, 182

Field, Joseph, 30

Field, Marshall, 31

"Fighting Wabash", 69

Finkbine, E. C., 188

Finkbine, W. O., 188

Fischer, Charles R., 124

Flagg, J. P., 45

Floyd City, Iowa, 18

Fonda, Iowa, 64, 71

Ford, Henry, 204

Fort Des Moines, Iowa, 1-2, 8, 11-12, 19, 21, 106, 139

Fort Dodge, Des Moines & Southern Railway, 92, 233

Fort Randall, South Dakota, 17

Frame, Francis, 52

Frame, William H., 52, 54

Fullerton, Robert, 188

Furlong & Baker Electric Company, 235

Furlong Machine Company, 236

Garmer & Stiles Company, 234

"Genoa" (Steamer), 17

Getchell, Gertrude, 180

Gilbertson, G. S., 217

Gilmore, C. W., 188
Goode, F. D., 213
Goode, Lowry W., 213
Gould, Jay, 2, 67-68, 70, 73, 76-77
Granger, Barlow, 9
"Gray Cloud" (Steamer), 17
Great Atlantic & Pacific Tea Company, 235
Great Northern Railroad, 127
Great Western Railroad, 88, 159
Greater Des Moines Committee, 91, 112
Greene County Gazette, 61
Greene County, Iowa, 62
"Greenleaf On Evidence" (Law), 43-44
Greenwood Park, 103, 144-145
Grefe, Henry, 188
Grocers Wholesale Company, 232, 236
Guernsey, Attorney, 151
Gulf & Interstate Railroad, 89
"Halsey", 13
Hamilton County, Iowa, 83
Hamilton & Talbott, 119
Hammer, Alderman, 146
Hanes, W. B., 217
Hanna, Mayor James R., 157
Harbach, L., 190
Harding, J. A., 154
Harvey, Iowa, 85
Hawarden, Iowa, 3
Hawkeye Marquette Cement Company, 234
Head House (Hotel), 108
Heardley, O., 80
Herring, Clyde L., 190, 204
Hewitt, Charles, 188
High Bridge, 80-81
Highland Park, 103
Highland Park College, 203
Hill, James J., 127
Hindel, Widow Margaret, 80

Hippee, George B., 190
Hippee, George M., 190
Historical Atlas of Iowa, 52
Holland, Kate, 14, 20, 22
"Holly System", 96
Holmes, Judge, 109
Home for the Aged, 5, 106, 112-113
Home Loan & Investment Co., 234
Home Savings Bank, 220
Hooper, 88
Hotel Fort Des Moines, 227
Howe, James F., 74
Howell, J. W., 188
Hubbell, Annie, 87-120
    Also see Annie Hubbell Booge
Hubbell Avenue
    See Avenue Frederick M. Hubbell
Hubbell, Beulah C.
    See Beulah C. Wachtmeister
Hubbell Building, 232, 238
Hubbell Brothers, Incorporated, 238
(Hubbell), Aunt Caroline, 46
Hubbell, Crawford C., 228
Hubbell Estate—See Trustees of the Frederick M. Hubbell Estate
Hubbell, F. M. Son & Company, Incorporated, 79, 99, 153, 210, 221, 237-238
Hubbell, Francis Burritt, 1, 11, 120, 127
Hubbell, Frances Cooper, 139-140, 185, 225
    Also see Frances Cooper
Hubbell, Fred Cooper, 60, 70-71, 79, 86, 89-90, 100, 122, 132, 137, 140-141, 145, 151-152, 160-161, 164-166, 186, 190, 208, 210, 229-230, 237

Hubbell, Frederick Marion, 1-6, 11, 23, 37-38, 53-54, 61-62, 65-67, 70, 73-74, 77-79, 86, 90-92, 94, 112, 119, 122-123, 125, 131, 133, 135, 137, 140-141, 143, 145, 160-161, 164, 168, 170-172, 175, 182-183, 187, 190, 196, 207, 222-223, 230-233, 236-239

Hubbell, Frederick W., 122, 137, 140-142, 151, 161, 164-165, 171, 178, 226, 237

Hubbell, Grover C., 131-134, 137, 140, 161, 164-165, 167, 171, 185, 230, 237-238

Hubbell, James W., 106, 137, 140-142, 151, 161, 164-165, 171, 225, 228-229, 237-238

Hubbell, Mrs. James W., 228

Hubbell Realty Company, 238

Hubbell, Solon, 18, 57

Hubbell Trust, 160, 167, 171

Hughes Barber Shop, 235

Hull, J. A. T., 190

Hume, J. C., 160

Hunt, Dr., 197

Hunter, E. H., 191, 202

Huntington, Connecticut, 6, 131

Hussey, Tacitus, 180

Huttenlocher, Chris, 145, 208

Ingham, Frances Cooper Hubbell, 140

Ingham, Harvey, 215

Insurance Exchange Building, 153, 210, 232, 234

Iowa Central Railroad, 88

Iowa City, Iowa, 8

Iowa Concrete Block & Material Company, 232

Iowa Loan & Trust Company, 99

Iowa Mutual Tornado Insurance Association, 234

Iowa National Bank, 215, 218

Iowa Radio Corporation, 236

Iowa Star, The, 9

Iowa State Register, 59, 67, 77, 180, 212, 215

Irving (Hotel), 8

Jackson, William, 80

Jamison, Mattie, 24, 26, 200

Jefferson, Iowa, 61, 64, 71, 108

Jeffries, Frank, 144

Jewett Building, 232

Jewett Lumber Company, 234

John Deere Plow Company of Moline, 232, 236

Jones, Senator George W., 14

Jones, William M., 100

Kansas City, Mexican & Orient Railroad, 89

Kauffman, B. F., 148, 150

Kelleher, T. J., 217

Keller, Helen, 203

Kelly, "General" Charles, 196

Kelly's Army, 196

Kent (Law), 43-44, 48

Keokuk, Iowa, 9

Keosauqua, Iowa, 23

Kewanee Boiler Company, 234

King, 149

Kinney, Judge, 191

Kirk, David, 228

Kirkwood Hotel, 232, 236

Knights Templar, 13

Knudson, William & Sons, Inc., 235

Kromer's Orchestra, 177

Kurtz, L. R., 217

Lagerquist Body Company, 233

Land Office, Sioux City, 14; United States, 2

Lawrenceville, New Jersey, 133

Leachman Lumber Company, 234

Lewis, 55

Life Insurance Institute, 122
Liljencrantz, Baron D., 180
Lincoln, Abraham, 203
Lindholm, Carrie C., 219
Lindholm, S. J., 219
Logan, Iowa, 19
London, Jack, 19
Long, Theodore K., 121
Love, H. K., 150
Lovejoy Construction Company, 235
M. & St. L. Railroad, 88
Macy, J. C., 154
Madrid, Iowa, 88
Magill, Mr., 203
Magnolia, Iowa, 13
Manila Bay, 127
Marengo, Iowa, 8
Marshalltown, Iowa, 158-159
Martin, L. M., 79
Meck, C. F., 80-81, 83
Meredith, E. T., 190, 217
Merrill, Samuel, 66
Methodist Hospital, 107, 112
Metropolitan Trust Company, 218
Metz, Wm. H. & Co., 235
Mid-Continent Petroleum Corporation, 235
Middle Sioux City, Iowa, 21
Miller, Homer, 218
Miller, Roswell, 87, 213
Mills, Pleasant J., 188
Milwaukee Railroad, 86, 90-91, 213
Mitchell, Alderman, 157
Mitchell, Ben, 80
Mitchell, W. F., 113
Monona County, Iowa, 15, 199
Moore, Dr., 129
Morris, A. Estate, 119
Murray, 55
Muscatine, Iowa, 8
Mutual Life Insurance Company of New York, 116

Mac Vicar, John, Sr., 144, 158
McCall, 48
McDonald, A. Y. Manufacturing Company, 235
McKinney, J. A., 221
McLaughlin, Cresswell, 192
Narrow Gauge Railway Construction Company, 67, 72-73
"Needles & Pins", 190
Nelson, Elmer, 224
Neumann, Arthur H. & Brothers, 234
New Monarch Machine & Stamping Company, 232, 234
Newman, Oliver, 175
Newton, Iowa, 8
Nollen, Henry S., 122
North Des Moines, Iowa, 143, 145, 151
North Des Moines Waterworks, 152-153
North Western Railroad, 64-66
Northeast Boulevard, 157
Northwestern Associated Press, 212
O'Dea Chevrolet Company, 236
"Ogden, E. A." (Steamer), 25
Ohio Falls, Car Works, 79
"Olympia" (Steamer), 138
"Omaha" (Steamer), 4, 39
Orange City, Iowa, 56
Owl Club, 187
Pacific City, Iowa, 19
Palmer, F. W., 59
Paramount Theater Building, 232
Park Bank, New York, 218
Parks, C. F., 150
Parrish, J. L., 91, 190
Payson, C. H., 153
Peoples Savings Bank (Cleveland, Ohio), 148

Perkins, Oliver H., 51, 150, 180, 192
Perry Creek, 25
Phillips Petroleum Company, 236
"Pigmaleon", 190
Pitman Shorthand, 43
Pittsburgh-Des Moines Steel Company, 232-233
Pittsburg Landing, 192
Plaine, Frank, 80
Polk County District Court, 166, 168
Polk County Treasurer, 236
Polk & Hubbell, 93, 99, 119, 173
Polk, Jefferson S., 57, 62, 65, 67, 73-74, 77, 94, 104, 119, 145, 190, 219, 230
Portland Cement Association, 234
Potter, H. C., 190
Potthoff & Rosene Company, 235
Pratt Paper Company, 233
Pray, G. B., 214
Prouty, C. C., 188
Prouty, Harry, 177
Pullman Company, 82
Pulsifer, E. F. & Company, 98
Raccoon River, 58
Rawson, Senator Charles E., 215
Red Oak Road, 112
Red Rock Coal Company, 101
Redhead, Wesley, 118, 230
Reese, Miss, 199
Register & Tribune, The, 215
Reigelman, Ida, 218
Reveries of a Bachelor, 30
Reynolds, Isham, 80
Reynolds, L. W., 80
Rich, J. M., 139
Richards Wilcox Manufacturing Company, 236
Roadside Settlement, 107, 112
Roberts, Phil, 80

Robinson, C. H., 191
Rock Island, Illinois, 8
Rock Island Railroad, 67
Rockwell, Mr., 173
Roe, Zell, 154-155
Rogers, Mary, 180
Rogg, Charles W., 190
Root Casket Company, 235
"Rowena" (Riverboat), 34
Runnells, John S., 67, 74, 81-82, 215
Runnells, Lucy, 177
Rustin, Charles B., 30-31, 37, 42
Sage, Russell, 2, 67, 70
St. Louis, Des Moines & Northern Railroad, 71, 80
St. Louis, Missouri, 68; Subtreasury, 10
St. Louis Union Trust Company, 218
St. Marks Memorial, 112
Sanborn, Dr., 197
Sargent, Fred, 190
Savery, J. C., 190
Schaetzle, Arnold, Attorney, 235
Schmidt, Jacob Brewing Company, 234
Schulze Baking Company, 234
Scranton, Iowa, Journal, 63, 69-70
Sharpe, Major Walter D., M.D., 139
Sheldon, 149
Sherman, Hoyt, 13, 97, 101, 118-120, 125-126, 173, 190, 199, 230
Sherman, Lampson, 13, 230
Sherman Paper Stock Company, 233
Simmons Company, The, 235
Sinclair Refining Company, 234
Sioux City, 3, 14-15, 19, 21-23, 43, 53, 125, 197-198, 200; Clerk of the District Court, 3, 38; Stockyards, 18

Sioux City Eagle, 44
Sioux County, Iowa, 3, 50, 52
Six Mile Creek, 55
Sloan Pierce Lumber Company, 236
Smith, Simpson P., 238
Smouse, Dr., 128
"Smutty Bear" (Indian Chief), 15
Spanish American War, 127
Standard Chemical Company, 235
Stewart, J. B., 190
Stone, A., 148
Stone, Emerson, 52, 54
Stoner-McCray System, 233
Story of Sioux County (Dyke), 53
Strauss, Samuel, 191
Superior Oil Company, 235
Supreme Court of Iowa, 167
Swedish Consul General (Cairo, Egypt), 137
Swedish Consul General (Havana, Cuba), 137
Swedish Consulate (Chicago), 136
Swedish Legation (Paris), 136
Tangney-McGinn, Inc., 236
Tanvilac Company, Inc., 235
Terrace Hill, 97, 114, 136-137, 140, 144, 164, 170-176, 181-183, 185-186, 189, 191, 196, 226, 232
Terrace Hill Inventory (Contents), 183-185
Texas Company, The, 235
Texas Southern Railroad, 89-90
Thomas Electric Company, 236
Thompson, H. D., 79, 100, 145, 151, 173, 177, 180, 208, 210, 230
Thompson, Mrs. H. D., 100
Thompson Trust, The, 210, 238

Tidrick, R. L., 119
Town Mutual Dwelling Insurance Company, 234
Trawver, C. J., 235
Trinity Churchyard, 81
Troy Laundry Company, 232-233
Trustees of the Frederick M. Hubbell Estate, 153, 210, 221, 238
Turner, Dr. Mahlon P., 94
Twentieth Century Fox Film Corporation, 235
Tyler, M., 14
"Umbria" (Steamer), 135
Underwood Corporation, 234
Union Carbide & Carbon Corporation, 233
Union Pacific, 64, 68
United Des Moines Clay Company, 235
United States Supreme Court, 91
Universal Film Exchange, 235
University Place, 144-145
University Place Church, 203
Valley National Bank, 219
VanEvera, George, 188
Victoria Hotel, 232
Victoria Hotel Company, 235
Virgil (Latin), 10, 27, 30, 36, 43
Wabash Railroad, 68, 73, 90-91
Wabash, St. Louis & Pacific Railroad, 69, 73
Wabash Syndicate, 72-73, 75
Wachtmeister, Beulah C., 103, 131, 134-136, 138, 161, 164-165, 167, 175-176, 218, 237
Wachtmeister, Count Carl A., 135-136, 138, 175-176
Wachtmeister, Fredrik H. C., 137
Wade, Martin, 189

262

Wagner, Jacob, 208
Wales House (Hotel), 191
Wallace, Henry C., 227
Warfield, W. R., 188
Warner Bros. Pict. Dist. Corp., 236
Watkins, Roy, 114
Weare's Claim, 20
Weaver, J. B., 239
Weitz, 149
Wellslager, R. T., 110
West, Fannie, 180
West, Mr. & Mrs. Harry, 180
West Point Military Academy, 7, 14, 56
Western Newspaper Union, 233
White, U. B., 94
Wilchinski, Norman, 91
Wilkins, Mary, 23-24, 37-39, 41
Wilson, Mary, 178
Wilson, Woodrow, 203-204

Windsor, J. H., 150-151, 180, 188-190
Windsor, Mary, 151
Windsor, Mary Belle Hubbell, 140
Windsor, Raymond, 177, 180
Wolin, M. A. Plumbing & Heating Company, 235
Woodbury County, Iowa, 16, 38, 41, 53; Warrants, 46
Woodland Cemetery, 230
Woodworth, 88
World War I, 106-107, 138, 141, 204-205
Wright County, Iowa, 83
Wright, George G., 190
Y. M. C. A., 107, 112
Y. W. C. A., 107, 112
Yale, 133-134
Young, Lafayette, 144
"Young's Farm", 80
Younkers, 210, 232, 235